MW01629557

The Fitness of Not Quitting

7 Strategies to Never Quit Fitness Again

Antonio D. Evans

The Fitness of not quitting

7 Strategies to Never Quit Fitness Again

Copyright@2021 Antonio D. Evans

All rights reserved. No portion of this book may be reproduced mechanically, electronically, or by any other means, including photocopying---without written permission from the author and publisher. For permission request, please write the publisher, addressed, "Attention: Permission Coordinator" at the address below.

Antonio D. Evans/ReShape Fitness LLC

P.O. Box 714

Reidville, SC 29375

ISBN: 978-0-9884102-0-6

Printed in the USA

DEDICATION

To my family, my extended team, and clients from all over that have pushed me towards growth, thank you. To God, a source of resources, I honor you. And to those that have quit along the way, I want to encourage you.

Praise for The Fitness of not Quitting

I have known Antonio Evans for more than 20 years, initially as an undergraduate taking my university courses and subsequently as a friend. Antonio is a sincere, honest, humble, and impressive individual. It is a great honor to me that he and I have had a confluence of our lives. Antonio has a knowledge base that has enabled him to achieve remarkable professional accomplishments and to undergo a continuing, stellar career in the fitness industry. Authoring this book is a superb accomplishment for Antonio and an important addition to the literature. I like how, in The Fitness of not quitting, Antonio describes the physiological importance of fitness on both the body and the mind.

Christopher M. DeWitt, Ph.D.
Professor and Chair
Department of Exercise and Sports Science
University of South Carolina Aiken

"Antonio is a man who knows and understands his purpose. He's a fitness leader and innovator who guide others to become their best selves. Antonio Evans knows firsthand what it means to never stop pursuing a dream and a life worth living."

Bethany Gainey
Sports Performance Coach
Auburn University

"Anyone looking for the right reasons to stick with fitness and mental conditioning strategies, Antonio gives them to you in this book."

Demetrius Jones
Founder of DJ Personal Fitness and Wellness

"Antonio Evans is the consummate fitness professional. He has a genuine passion for helping others reach their health and fitness goals by training the mind and the body with an emphasis on self-love, self-care, and self-acceptance, as you will read in Chapter 1."

Sophia Marshall,
Sr. Associate Director, University Recreation at the University of North Carolina at Charlotte

---

"As a Kenyan runner, I know first-hand the importance of the mental conditioning Antonio speaks so highly of in his book. He's a great motivator!"

Amos Kimutai, Kenyan Runner, Entrepreneur

Table of Contents

FOREWORD BY

Dr. Carl A. Foulks Jr. MD

As someone who indulges in quite a bit of nonfiction reading, I came across a book that identified certain individuals as "connectors". The definition in the book was an individual who was your initial connection that led you to establish your social circle. When it comes to the role that Antonio played as a connector in my life, he was the one who connected me to a much healthier lifestyle that I continue to lead over 15 years later. As someone who played sports as a kid, I was never considered a "couch potato". As a medical student and a resident, I would only go to the gym intermittently and move a few weights up and down. Every so often, I would play the occasional pickup game of racquetball or basketball, with no consistency. Fortunately, genetics and youthful metabolism never let my weight get out of control.

After finishing the 14 years of training/education it took to become a practicing physician, I was tasked with starting a new practice just outside of Charlotte and the stresses of the job, combined with a poor diet and a pack a day smoking habit, led to significant weight gain and low-energy levels. I knew I needed to workout and eat better, but didn't have the discipline at the time to do it by myself. Enter Antonio Evans; in 2008, he was working with a fitness company in Cornelius that offered in-home training, which was perfect for my schedule. Antonio met with me and came up with a personalized program to get me on the right track. His knowledge, enthusiasm, and professionalism inspired me to stay on task and power through the progressively tougher workouts on my schedule. We also became fast friends, and I would look forward to the motivational chats I would have with him on the days I swing by his gym and grab a chocolate smoothie with rolled oats on my way home from work.

Over the next several months, I went on to lose 30lbs of fat and gain 10lbs of lean muscle. By this time, I had adopted a lifestyle that not only incorporated fitness and good nutrition into my daily routine, but it became an effective way to motivate my patients to adopt healthier habits to improve their medical conditions. In a profession as a gastroenterologist where recommendations for proper nutrition and lifestyle changes are part of my daily discourse with patients, leading by example has been monumentally helpful when counseling them and has helped me to improve countless outcomes. In addition to facilitating my ability to help my patients lead healthier lives, I went on to complete an Iron Man, climb Mount Kilimanjaro, and finish an ultramarathon in the desert outside Las Vegas.

When you trace my personal fitness journey back to the individual who inspired me to get off my ass and start moving, I have Antonio to thank for being my "wellness connector". He got me on track to accomplish things I never would have imagined that I could have achieved. This gave me the ability to not only "talk the talk", but "walk the walk" when it comes to counseling my patients on nutrition and exercise. As you read the pages that follow, I am confident that you'll be inspired as I was, and always remember that when reshaping your body, you will be both the sculptor and the stone, this may hurt a bit… Good luck.

Dr. Carl A. Foulks, Jr., MD

THE FITNESS OF NOT QUITTING

7 Strategies to Never Quit Fitness Again

How often do you start and stop things? Like meditation, going to the gym, goal setting, working out at home, eating healthier, drinking more water, etc. There's both an art and science to fitness. It's a weapon of choice for those that can see the unlimited benefits. Your sitting posture and confidence at a job interview can be attributed to your fitness. Your ability to handle stress at home or at work could be a benefit from exercising. Not quitting on your fitness can often be related to not quitting other things in life. Where's your stick-to-itiveness?

As you search your inner being for reasons to stay the course and finish what you've started, found in this book are 7 strategies to implement for betterment.

1. Love yourself enough to love yourself some more (change starts here).
2. Condition your mind daily for the journey.
3. Have an earth-shaking reason that will keep you focused.
4. Break down your goals into three sizes (small, medium, and large).

5. Simplify the process to maintain consistency every week.

6. Rely on your accountability team… the people who want to see you win.

7. Celebrate small victories to build motivation.

Fitness is very relatable; it is life-long and downright good for you. Stay true to your physical conditioning and watch how it positively impacts other areas of your life. Who cares if most people throw in the towel on their exercise regimen? This doesn't have to be you. Since we know diets don't work, but lifestyle changes do, make the needed adjustments and live well. Find your "why" and you will have a foundation for long-term success. You can work out three times a week consistently by "Winning the Day". We know that quitting is contagious, but so is finishing. The Fitness of Not Quitting is about your mental strength just as much as your physical. The body is willing, but it's the mind that gets weak. So, the reality is, both can and should be strong. May your "I'm not quitting" mindset kick in sooner than later, and perhaps you can stay afloat until you learn how to swim, but don't quit.

See you on the other side of a great workout!

INTRODUCTION: WHY YOU SHOULD NOT QUIT

What's the problem as I see it? We quit way too often and way too easily. Not just on our fitness, but on life. Why do we quit things that are of value to us? With help in answering this powerful question, I'll lend my 20 years of training and coaching clients as experience for a generalized answer.

1. Low self-esteem.
2. Fear of failure or success.
3. Not knowing what we want.
4. Lack of focus and consistent action.

We all have goals and some of those include career success, personal ambition and fitness targets. We want to accomplish something we can be proud of at the end of the day. It feels good to make maximum use of our gym membership. Not only that, but we want to stick to a healthy nutrition plan and workout even when we're confined to our homes. Furthermore, we have the determination and the passion to do great things. But sometimes, something comes up just when we've started and stops us. Other times, we stop when we're halfway there or just when we're about to make it. Then we lose sight of our goals, and we quit for too long. Then, we're forced to start all over again. Because physical fitness is a key element of well-being, I encourage you to make it a top priority. Regardless of our busy schedules, it's still possible to find time and fit in at least 30 minutes of exercise a day.

A major factor that causes many people to abandon their fitness program is failure to see physical results as soon as they would like to see them. After a few workout sessions, most people are eager to see dramatic changes, but the truth is it takes time to produce results. In most cases, the changes are already happening, though you can't notice anything yet. The health benefits of exercise begin after your first workout. Consistency is what brings long-term, visible results. Hopefully, this is the impetus you need to stick to your fitness routine.

Did you know that your fitness can have a significant impact on other aspects of your life? It affects your self-confidence, self-esteem, and mental health. There are many benefits of staying fit.

Alert Mind

A fit body contributes to a healthier mind. This is because regular physical activity increases blood flow to the brain and improves mental processes, boosting overall brain function. All exercises have a beneficial effect on the brain; however, aerobic exercise has been proven to have the greatest impact on mental sharpness. Aim to engage in exercises like walking, swimming, cycling or running to get your heart rate up. Did you know listening to music while you exercise further increases mental stimulation?

Stress Relief

Science has proven that physical activity can make you happier. Exercise regulates hormone levels, which can improve metabolism and reduce stress levels. It also activates the release of feel-good neurotransmitters like serotonin, endorphins, and dopamine to boost your mood soon after you engage in moderate exercise. Keep your exercises consistent with good intensity and varied to help keep your hormones balanced. Doing this also boosts your overall health.

We now know that exercises such as jogging, swimming, cycling and similar activities are very beneficial to your heart and lungs. These activities also have many benefits to help combat stress. Regular exercise reduces cortisol levels. Cortisol is a stress hormone. When your cortisol levels are down, you'll be less stressed. Exercise regulates your sleep patterns, enables relaxation by regulating your breathing patterns and relaxes your mind, alleviating the effects of anxiety.

This particular effect on your tension level is incredibly far-reaching. It helps you perceive unhealthy triggers differently, such that you become more resilient with time. As you maintain consistency in your routine, you'll notice less anxiety, less irritability and higher energy levels. Anytime you feel tense or annoyed by something which is out of your control, a yoga session or a jog around the block can be enough to relax you and clear your mind. Every time you make it through a challenging workout, your mind, and body react by becoming better at handling every kind of challenge.

The same benefit can be actualized whenever you resist the urge to reach out for that extra chocolate bar or a loaded burger that could interfere with your eating plan. When you stop yourself from going against the rules, you'll be able to make firm decisions in other areas of your life. You won't give in to temptations that could mess you up. It all begins with training your mind to follow the path you've set, whether it's in your exercise routine or your work schedule. The way you condition your brain to handle challenges enhances the natural growth of your resilience over time.

The fact that there are so many wonderful perks that come with choosing not to quit should inspire you to continue despite what gets in your way. You have a chance to start afresh. It's never too late; every new day signifies another chance for you. Take time to deal with whatever had caused you to quit, and you'll see a major improvement in all aspects of your life! As you become inspired, keep an understanding that there are many other benefits of staying fit. Let's examine some more of them:

Strengthening Your Immune System

Exercise balances your hormones, reduces chronic inflammation on a cellular level and helps to lower your blood pressure. It provides an all-around boost for many body functions. As little as 20 minutes of moderately intense exercise in a day can be beneficial, so you can start small and build your way up. It's not about where you start, but where you can go. Exercise wards off illnesses by maintaining a healthy metabolism, helping in weight management and protecting your immune system. You can avoid chronic issues like osteoporosis and arthritis, which usually affects older adults, by sticking to your workout routine. Working out sustains a lean muscle mass, which can prevent chronic diseases. The best results come when you incorporate a healthy nutrition strategy, and not forgetting drinking lots of water. This nourishes your body by providing everything you need to stay fit and healthy.

Improving Productivity

Exercise poses a challenge for your body and mind. To breathe correctly, to activate the right parts of your body, and to remain focused throughout a workout session, you naturally use your mind-muscle connection. This plays a key role in developing mental strength to accomplish more. Your brain is always working behind the scenes. Learn to harness the power of your mind.

Engaging your brain in exercise will reflect in your social, personal and professional life and help you improve your focus and problem-solving skills. In turn, you'll be able to do more in less time and eventually become more productive and able to reach your goals. Productivity and success will be evident in everything you do.

Did you know that every fitness decision you make is not limited to your physical appearance? Truth is, the more you commit yourself to exercise and eating healthy, the more you'll notice other positive changes in your life. Regardless of how long you've stayed without doing physical activity, this truth can motivate you to start again and stay consistent.

Increase Your Life Expectancy

Research has shown that regular exercise increases life expectancy and reduces the risk of premature death. There is no magic formula that translates hours of working out into years of life added, but research indicates that people who are more active are typically healthier and live longer. Do the necessary work!

Reducing Your Risk of Injury

Regular exercise and strength training boost muscle strength, bone density, flexibility, and stability. Being physically fit can reduce your risk for accidental injuries, especially as you get older. For example, better balance and stronger muscles mean that you're less likely to slip and fall, and stronger bones mean that you're less likely to suffer bone injuries if you fall. View it as injury prevention or injury recovery.

Improving the Quality of Your Life

A sedentary lifestyle can have a negative effect on your body. Being inactive is linked to an increased risk for certain types of cancer, many chronic illnesses and some mental health issues. Exercise improves mood and mental awareness and keeps your energy balanced. Unquestionably, it is a tool for an improved quality of life.

Remember that your body needs to rest occasionally. Too much exercise can result in fatigue and stress, leading to an imbalance of hormones. Recovery is a fundamental key to the unlimited rewards of exercise. Learn to rest when you need, as that is when the magic happens. Move your body, but also listen to it as well.

Learn to Enjoy the Journey

Fitness will never become a lifestyle if you hate the process. Let's fix that by adapting and adjusting to a new way of looking at health. Your mind and body is an asset that only you can determine the true value. Make fitness fun. You still have to sweat and work hard, but those things can be rewarding, as we know. Visible results may not show right away, so if you can learn to enjoy the journey, you are more likely to stay on board. With the right system, this should lead to lasting results and lifelong healthy habits.

In the next chapters, we'll look at the seven strategies you can start applying to improve your journey today.

"I can live better, I can give more, and I can heal when I learn to love myself. Change is an inside job, too. You can outgrow old versions of yourself. That's love!"

The Warm-up

JOURNEY ONE:

LOVE YOURSELF ENOUGH TO LOVE YOURSELF SOME MORE

Physical fitness is a witness, a bridge over trouble water, a symbol of strength, if you will. Some describe it as a condition that helps us look, feel, and do our best. On a deeper level, it's our ability to perform daily tasks vigorously and alertly, with energy left over to enjoy leisure time activities and meeting emergency demands. It is the ability to endure, to bear up, to withstand stress, to carry on in circumstances where unfit people could not continue, and is a major basis for good health and well-being. It is an expression of love. Fitness varies from individual to individual, and that's where the warm-up begins...with you!!

Have you ever tried the three-minute mirror test?

If not, it is a highly recommended exercise on your self-discovery journey. Here it is in a nutshell:

Go stand in the mirror and stare at yourself for 3 minutes, noticing all the remarkable things about you. Be sure to take physical and mental notes of what you see. For some, this is the first step to learning how to love who they are. This is the most important part of the warm-up thus far. Do you feel the love? I remember listening to a song in college titled "Because I love you" by Lenny Williams. What was striking about this love ballad was the passion in which he sang the song. As a listener, you could feel it. As I examined the lyrics in the song, it has a lesson about love that we can apply daily. He opened the song with an ooh, and an ahh to get you feeling the love. Now, for experiencing self-love, pretend you are singing the following lyrics to yourself, "(Insert your name), you know I, I, I, I love you, no matter what you do, and I hope you understand me, every word I say is true. Cause' I love you." What if we love ourselves with that type of passion and care? I mean, the man literally said "I" four times!! If reading it doesn't exude the passion you were hoping for, I recommend you go to YouTube, watch and listen. The point is we must learn to truly love who we are and who we hope to become. Often, when we abandon our fitness, we've actually taken a rest break from loving ourselves the way we should.

Self-love is vital if you want to succeed in anything you do, including staying fit. Loving yourself doesn't mean you're self-centered. It means you show compassion to yourself first before spreading it to others. Self-love should reflect even in your physical fitness, not just in the way you dress, eat or treat yourself. As humans, what we want can be summed up in these four ways, according to Phil Kaplan:

1. We want to feel good (Love).
2. We want to change positively (Love).
3. We want to be empowered (Love).
4. We want to know achievement and potential (Love).

Let's look at the story of Jack. He became a fitness fanatic in his younger years, and this continued throughout his high school and college days. He would play sports, jog and do several structured workouts every week. In fact, he exceeded the recommended 150 minutes of moderate activity per week. Jack was physically fit and had a body many admired. He rarely got sick, apart from rare instances of a minor cold or flu, which he quickly recovered from. Furthermore, he ate right and enjoyed good health. Jack kept his body hydrated, and not once did he miss his workout sessions.

Then soon after finishing college, Jack found an internship as a marketing rep in a big company. He followed his fitness routine while working as an intern, and afterwards, he was offered a permanent position as a marketing manager. With the lucrative nature of his career, Jack became extremely busy (but not too busy to take care of himself). He was earning good money, driving a nice car and living in a luxurious apartment downtown. As time went on, he was so excited and engrossed in his new lifestyle that he started missing his workout sessions. Evening meetings kept him occupied until night-time, and the demanding nature of his career made him wake up earlier than usual almost every morning. He lost the motivation to cook when he got back home. The majority of the time, he would buy ready-made or quick-serve food which is often loaded with calories, sugar, sodium and unhealthy fat. Many of his meals consisted of fries, burgers, hot-dogs and pizzas. He only had nutritious meals once or twice a week.

After a few months, Jack started gaining weight. He didn't notice this it because he was always busy. By now, he had completely quit his fitness routine for more than two months. He only realized what was happening to him when his clothes started getting a little tighter and when a colleague commented about his weight gain. That particular evening, Jack paused at his desk and recalled the bad life changes he had made over the past year. His fitness had disappeared, and now Jack is carrying excess belly fat. He had begun experiencing trouble sleeping. Oftentimes, he woke up feeling tired and fatigued. This was a sign of a slowing metabolism, weight gain, poor sleep habits, and unhealthy way of living.

Jack was not happy about how he had lost the athletic body so many of his friends admired. Although he has a good job and earns a respectable income, everything else was unpleasant in his life. He began experiencing full-blown fatigue coupled with bouts of depression. The minute he got a spell of dizziness while he was driving home after work, he knew he had to do something fast to regain his health and fitness.

Did Jack love himself? Perhaps he did, but he wasn't showing it. Maybe you can relate… Life has a way of hitting until it hurts. Jack wanted to have a good life and start his family soon. He also wanted to overcome depression and be happy again. He didn't want unwise lifestyle changes to get in the way of that. So, he made that life-changing decision to get the help he so much needed. He first went to see a counselor, who scheduled therapy and counseling sessions to help improve his mental health. Then Jack signed up for a gym membership at a nearby gym. He knew that if it was in proximity, there's a high likelihood that he would use it regularly. Jack found a good fitness trainer who would educate, motivate, and challenge him to improve in every aspect of fitness and wellness.

Jack faithfully attended his counseling, therapy and gym sessions. He organized his work schedule in such a way that it didn't interrupt his self-care routine. He realized he could set priorities at work and that some things would have to wait. Not only that, he even utilized a personal assistant who would complete some tasks when he was not around. A few months after Jack decided to turn around his life for the better, he began seeing a change. His body was getting back in shape. He was now enjoying good mental strength. The depression slowly disappeared and exercise became the medicine of choice. Even the fatigue that had almost cost him his job faded away. His friends and colleagues were once again admiring him for being in great shape and the way he was efficiently performing at work. Jack's fitness became a weapon that helped him excel as a manager achieving unprecedented growth and being a leader to his team. Do you remember those four things every human wants? They can be found in Jack's story and, if truth be told, in your story as well. The following year, the company Jack was working with set a record with a big leap in revenue, something they had not seen in the past 5 years. The board knew this success had a lot to do with Jack's productivity, leadership, and efficiency. They recognized his efforts and awarded him with a promotion. Two years later, another promotion would follow, naming him Head of Marketing. Jack was making his impact felt with the company, and three years after his last promotion, he would take over as CEO of the company!

Jack was elated as well as motivated. His entire life was taking an impressive turn. He had just become a CEO, and he was currently engaged to a beautiful, intelligent lady he had met at the gym. Even with all these achievements, Jack continued with his fitness routine. He chose nutritious meals and went for medical checkups twice a year. Jack is now a 45-year-old father of two, and he still balances family, work and self-care. He has kept his promise of never quitting. He found his "why." Now he and his family are enjoying the benefits of better choices.

We can learn a lot from Jack's story. Of course, he loved himself, but when he got a job, he forgot to love himself some more. He only focused on what was convenient for him — including his meals and work schedule. He forgot to prioritize his physical and mental well-being. His choices took a toll on his overall health, affecting many areas of his life. At some point, he almost couldn't go to work, but he made a turn-around early enough to recover and be promoted as the CEO.

This shows it's not too late for you to make a change. Self-love is simple, yet complicated, but this is where change starts. Prioritizing your fitness is a way of showing how much you love yourself. There may be other important areas in your life that need commitment, but your health comes first. It's your greatest wealth. Without good physical fitness, it will be hard for you to perform daily task at a high level. Exercise can affect many other areas of your life, including your social and professional life; that's why you need to prioritize your well-bring. If Jack hadn't realized this in time, he would have fallen sick and probably lost his job. His life would have taken a downward turn, and chances of him finding a good life partner would be low. So instead of letting wrong choices ruin our health and careers, let's continue to put high value on fitness, and it will bring other good things and achievements to our lives. Jack's story is just a gentle reminder of how life can get in the way quickly, and move us in the wrong direction on the journey towards total wellness. Build a solid foundation so when turbulence comes, you can withstand uncertainty and change. With this strategy, your fitness and wellness will be a resource in any situation. You won't see self-love promoted as a tool for not quitting, but trust me, it's immeasurable.

The Benefits of Self-Love

Self-love gives you tremendous benefits that can help you become more successful in anything you set out to do. Research has revealed the incredible social, psychological, and physical health benefits associated with self-love:

1. It increases motivation.

Loving yourself can increase your motivation to recover from failure, according to research. This is because you accept and acknowledge your weaknesses, and when you make up your mind to change and become better, you'll treat yourself kindly during the process. So if you were unable to finish that walk, or if you bowed out of your strength training class just before the end, don't beat yourself up for it. Accept that you failed and find ways you can do better next time.

2. Self-love boosts happiness.

Self-compassion is linked to better moods and positive characteristics. If this is new to you, just keep dancing until you find the rhythm. It's all love! Additionally, showing self-compassion is associated with happiness, optimism, wisdom, and personal initiative.

3. It improves body image.

Multiple studies have linked self-love to a healthier body image. This means that people who love themselves are not ashamed of their bodies, even if they are still improving their body composition. Such people experience less preoccupation with their appearance, fewer worries about weight, and a greater appreciation for who they are. When you accept your body the way it is, you won't be preoccupied with worry, so you'll fully focus on doing exercise to get back in shape.

4. Self-love improves self-worth.

In today's world, high self-esteem often depends on external circumstances and social comparisons; true self-love comes from within. Self-love enables you to continue feeling worthy despite knowing that you've failed at some point and despite having feelings of imperfection. When you know your worth, you know yourself.

5. It makes you resilient during hard times.

Being kind to yourself can play a key role in helping you navigate through tough times. People who get back on their feet after having to endure hardship are often those who love themselves. In their minds, love is powerful enough to know that they deserve another chance.

6. Self-love improves your mental health.

People who practice self-compassion are less likely to experience mental health problems. In doing so, it reduces feelings of anxiety and depression. As a result of showing self-love, this allows you to do the things that are good for you, such as staying fit and choosing supportive meals.

Made With and For Love

You now know why you need to practice self-love, despite the storms you might have gone through in the past. You can stop dwelling on your mistakes immediately and see a positive turnaround.

If you think you've never been good enough, you will realize how wrong you've been when you start treating yourself with a little more love. Accepting yourself for who you are will help you to become better. There are some things you can do to make it easy to take a more self-compassionate approach. Start with talking to yourself like you would speak to a trusted friend. While you're at it, train your mind to be supportive when you're trying to recover from difficult situations. Saying kinder things to yourself will not only help you feel better, but it will also help you perform better.

We also learned that sometimes we might have to reschedule our routines when change comes. While we adapt to becoming better, let's consider the current improvements in our lives, keeping in mind that change is about adjustments. Whether it's a new job or new fitness class, we can make a favorable schedule that helps us continue to grow. Be fluid like water. If you need to reset the time you usually do your workouts, don't hesitate, as long as you find consistency. Do you want to have family time and get fit? Consider working out together.

Hopefully, you can understand the value and power of self-love and how it can play a role in sticking to fitness or any life endeavor. As you continue to gain a greater appreciation for who you are, there are 4 powerful questions that, if answered truthfully and with detail, can ascend you to new heights. The order in which the questions are asked resonates with the inner power you begin to gain from answering them.

Powerful Questions

1. Who are you? (Subject)
2. What do you want? (The desires of your heart)
3. Why do you want it? (Your why)
4. How will you get it? (Your action plan or strategy)

The gathering of information is always fundamental when seeking answers and creating a blueprint. The cool thing with this exercise is you are the subject. The deeper you dive, the more you arrive. When we hear the question "who are you?" we often think about our name, where we are from, maybe what we do for a living. This powerful question is not for answers of that sort. At your core being, who are you? If you ask most people what they want, they probably can't give a direct answer. The question "What do you want?" gives you all the space you desire to express yourself. If you told me you want to be healthy and wealthy, I would immediately ask why… This is your time to shine by truthfully knowing why you want something. Finally, you arrive at "How". This is your plan of action to get what you want out of any aspect of life. Take your time with each question and be uniquely you in answering them. The journey continues…here's what you can start doing right now.

Action Steps:

1. Put your health and fitness at the top of your priorities.
2. Use fitness as a weapon to accomplish more in life.
3. Say, think, and do good things for the betterment of you.
4. Monitor and adjust accordingly.

"My mind is a muscle that I choose to condition because I believe it is a superpower and can help me in any situation. The stronger it becomes, the more I can flourish."

JOURNEY TWO:

CONDITION YOUR MIND DAILY FOR THE JOURNEY

Since betterment is a life goal, and we are on a journey of improvement, it is important to get our minds prepared for battle. Trust, it will be a fight until you master your mind. Once we've conditioned our minds for success, we are better equipped to finish and not quit. By the way, what do we typically quit? Well, that depends on each individual, but I will give a short list that is likely universal to mankind to some degree. We quit:

—Growing Spiritually

—Believing in Ourselves

—Dreaming

—Important Life Projects

—Fitness Programs

—Preparing for the Future

While this is a short list, you've likely quit more than half of the areas listed at some point. Do a quick scan over your life and see what you have quit that was meaningful and had the potential to be impactful had you stayed the course. Remember, I'm not talking about things that were not good for you or your well-being, but things you knew you should have completed or maintained. As you get that visual in your head, let me introduce you to your EEM. This is your Emotional Experimental Memory, and it plays a key role in our thinking and consequently, our doing. In particular, experiences we've deemed as failure. It acts as a protector or safety net. If the stove is hot, your EEM warns you not to touch it. This is a good communication sensor to have, but it also plays a similar role when we make attempts at starting over or taking risks in life. Let's say you started working out, and your muscles were sore for 4 days, so you stop working out because you prefer not to feel that way ever again. That's your EEM talking. It probably sounds similar to this in your head, "You know how much pain you were in last time and could barely make it to work. Don't do that again" So now you have deemed the experience as a failure and your EEM pushes you back to safety. Maybe you were not armed with the right information of a proper warm-up, a beginner's program, a proper cool-down, and stretching. Perhaps, knowing that recovery modalities like foam rolling could help decrease muscle soreness and speed up recovery would have prompted you to stick with it. Your EEM doesn't care about anything I just mentioned, but your PFC does. This is what's called your Prefrontal Cortex, aka the adventure seeker, challenge taker, thrilla in Manila, if you may. If you replay the same scenario from above, this is likely what your PFC would say, "Wow, I can tell it's been a while since I have done a workout, but I'm looking forward to the next one." This is the type of mental conditioning you will need to enhance your stick-to-itiiveness. Jack showed it, and you will soon see how Sheila displayed it as well.

Getting back on track will require having a new frame of mind. The way we think is everything. It will determine how you feel and what you do. For example, when change comes, and you develop the wrong mindset, perhaps because you're doubtful or hesitant to take on new responsibilities, you won't use the right strategies to navigate through the situation. In Jack's case, he was too excited about his new job that he underestimated the importance of staying fit. He started believing getting enough exercise wasn't that necessary anymore because he had entered a new phase in his life. He was hesitant to adjust his schedule, and he ended up neglecting fitness altogether. Jack developed the wrong mentality until negative effects began troubling him. That's when he realized he had to be responsible for his well-being.

You don't have to wait until you find yourself in Jack's situation. Even if you've neglected your fitness for a while, you can start embracing the right mindset now. Start eliminating negative thoughts and allow positive ones to be birthed. A good line of thinking can give you the will to start again and make the necessary changes so that you don't have to quit, no matter what's going on in your life. Start by putting positive thoughts in your mind daily. When it comes to finding motivation, positivity is the key. Think about all the benefits of staying fit, as we learned in the introduction.

The fact that fitness can improve both your physical and mental health should be enough to keep you motivated. Besides, you get to expand your social circle, and thanks to technology, you can stay connected with your fitness community even when it's not possible to meet physically. Did you know having people you can share your health journey with empowers you? It does so by giving you access to support when you need it. Furthermore, it gives you a chance to encourage others. And reminds you every day that you're not the only one who is going through this process — there are many others like you, and you are all aiming to stick to your routines.

As you embark on your fitness journey, remember there will be obstacles. These challenges can stem from various aspects of life. What are you going to do when it is pouring rain, and you've had a long day at work? Will you workout? If mental conditioning is a part of your success strategy, you will. Don't let obstacles stall your breakthrough. I strongly believe that for every problem, there is a solution. Whatever comes your way, find a way around it or through it. Get help if you need to. Unsolved problems can pile up and stop you from making progress in life — or in your fitness. Issues at work, in your personal life or in your family should be dealt with so that you can have the right frame of mind on your journey.

Let's read the story of Sheila and see how she overcame obstacles to succeed as a working mother. By the age of 22, Sheila had just finished studying Public Relations, and she was now employed by a top telecommunications company. At college, she had met an attractive guy named Phil. They were in a romantic relationship and from the way things were going; Sheila was sure they would become engaged, married and live happily. Phil didn't show any signs of leaving her, so she gave him her whole heart. He was honest with her. He even took her to meet his parents. And she did the same. She was expecting a proposal anytime, but what came immediately afterwards was anything but expected. Sheila found out she was pregnant. She had never talked about it with Phil. It happened so unexpectedly that she found it hard to disclose the news to Phil. She wasn't sure how he would react.

Sheila knew her life was taking a different turn. She would need financial support because she had barely settled in her new permanent job. She also knew her schedule would change at some point. Sheila had grown accustomed to working out at least 3 times a week. Furthermore, she wasn't sure if or how she would stick to that routine as months progressed.

When Sheila finally got the courage to disclose the news to Phil, the answers she got left her with mixed feelings. Phil was a bit surprised to hear about the pregnancy, but he promised to support her both financially and emotionally. He, however, insisted that he was not ready for marriage. He said he was only 23, a year older than her, and he needed more time to 'get it together'. Whatever that meant! Sheila was disappointed to learn that they couldn't get married yet, but she was relieved to know he would always be there whenever she needed him. He had accepted responsibility. That was better than nothing. Sheila couldn't imagine how she would have felt if he refused to support her. She was somehow happy she wouldn't go through her pregnancy journey alone.

Throughout her childhood and into young adulthood, Sheila had always had a slender, athletic body, which she loved. She had stuck to her fitness routine all along, and she didn't want anything to stop her from reaching her goals. Now that she was pregnant, she knew she would change the way she exercised. No more horse-riding or bungee jumping. Mountain climbing would be risky too. Sheila would still need to be on the move during pregnancy, but she had to keep it simple. Before starting a whole new exercise routine, Sheila decided to consult her doctor first.

She had read somewhere that pregnant women who exercise have less back pain, more energy, a better body image and, post-delivery, a faster return to their pre-pregnancy shape.

Other benefits are:

- Keeping your mind and body strong. Physical activity can help you feel good and give you extra energy. It also strengthens your heart, lungs, and blood vessels.
- It helps you gain the right amount of weight during pregnancy.
- Ease some common discomforts of pregnancy like constipation, back pain and swelling in your legs, ankles, and feet.
- It helps you manage stress and sleep better.
- Reduces the risk of pregnancy complications like gestational diabetes and preeclampsia. Gestational diabetes is a kind of diabetes that occurs during pregnancy. It happens when there is too much sugar in the blood. Preeclampsia is a type of high blood pressure some women get after the 20th week of pregnancy or after giving birth. These conditions can increase your risk of having complications during pregnancy, such as premature birth.

- Reduces the risk of having a cesarean birth.
- Prepares the body for labor and birth. Engaging in activities like prenatal yoga can help you practice breathing, meditation and other calming methods that may help you manage labor pain. Regular exercise can help give you the energy and strength to get through labor.

Sheila wanted all of that. She wanted to maintain her athletic body, even if her life was taking a new turn. Dr. Freddie gave her valuable advice and encouraged her to maintain a work-life balance and get all the support she needed. This would help keep her comfortable. She would also have a smooth pregnancy journey, even if it happened unexpectedly. Sheila would need at least 2½ hours of aerobic activity, such as walking or swimming, every week. Because she was familiar with more intense workouts, that wouldn't be hard to achieve. She was happy that the doctor had given her the go-ahead to continue exercising. (Exercise is not safe for some women during pregnancy; it's best to seek a doctor's advice as soon as you discover you're pregnant.)

Sheila did low-impact, simple exercises under the guidance of her trainer. She wore loose-fitting shoes and didn't exercise to the point of exhaustion. At the end of each workout, she felt better and refreshed. Phil supported her as the months went by until she finally started maternity leave. Everything was going well. She had a healthy baby boy. Phil and the rest of her family were excited. Phil continued to support her in every way. Then things changed when their son turned 6 months old. Sheila hired a nanny so that she could go back to work. All of a sudden, Phil became distant and stopped supporting her financially. He said his sales job was no longer paying well, so he couldn't provide for Sheila and their son. She could only depend on her job (which was not paying well) to take care of the baby, pay her nanny and settle other bills.

Sheila felt that Phil was lying to her. It was like he didn't love her anymore. Her suspicions about Phil proved to be true when one evening she spotted him in a convertible with another lady. They were both laughing as they sped by. Phil didn't seem to be depressed, as he had claimed when Sheila spoke to him on the phone. Sheila felt devastated that she almost slipped into depression. She had resumed her fitness routine, but now she couldn't get herself to do even the simplest exercise. Her mind kept going back to Phil and the lies he was telling her. She wondered why he had changed so suddenly. Didn't he care about her and their son anymore? Sheila couldn't find answers to her questions.

She barely got along at work. She only spent a few hours with her son. Then she started gaining weight. The stress she was experiencing was becoming almost too much to handle. That's when she knew she needed help. She was in a dark place, and she had to get out as fast as possible. It was also necessary to get back to her fitness routine and restore her athletic body. Sheila acted before it was too late. She talked to a renowned therapist who helped her cope with depression and eventually overcame it. Her fitness trainer was also very helpful. Within a few months, Sheila had found happiness from within herself and her body was back in shape. She spared enough time to spend with her now one-year-old son. She also visited her family more often. Sheila began noticing the things that really matter in life — a happy family, peace of mind, support, and a sense of belonging.

Phil decided to start another life without her. Sheila made up her mind to let him be. She wouldn't force him to stay. Instead, she focused on the journey ahead — taking care of her son, succeeding in her career and sticking to her fitness routine. It wouldn't be an easy journey, but with the right support, she would make it. She would have to balance her time between family, work, and fitness. This would include other self-care activities. Sheila conditioned her mind for the journey she was venturing into. She was ready to deal with any challenge that would come her way. Likewise, she adjusted her schedule and only took on the number of tasks she could manage at a time. Sheila didn't overwhelm herself, nor did she do too little. She learned to give her all in everything she did. The excellent results that came afterwards impressed her boss, and soon her salary increased exponentially. Sheila didn't struggle to take care of her son anymore. Her life became more comfortable. She could move to a better apartment and buy a brand-new car. Still, it wasn't easy managing everything as a single mother, but every morning she reminded herself that she was meant to succeed.

This daily reminder became her inspiration. It was more of an affirmation, helping her develop the right mental conditioning and prepare her mind for what was ahead. With this affirmation in mind, Sheila could face challenges at work and at home. When her babysitter quit the job, and she had to find someone new to help look after her son, this was just another challenge for Shelia. The desire to make everything work out motivated Sheila to be patient until she found the right person. Soon everything was running smoothly and Sheila's career thrived. Her son was happy. Her family was happy. And so was she. As life progressed, Sheila was glad she sought help when she did and not later when everything would be nearly falling apart.

Sheila's story could be similar to yours, but even if it's not, you can still learn something from her. She didn't let disappointments ruin her life. Although she felt the pain of not getting married to the man she loved, she got back up and made things work. She overcame life's obstacles by changing her mindset right in the nick of time.

More importantly, she didn't do it alone. She found the right support. That's why she could get back on her feet faster than she expected.

You, too, can change your mind despite what you're going through. It could be a personal problem, a family issue, or unfavorable conditions at work. Nothing should stop your progress. With support, you can sail through any kind of storm and get your power back. Success begins in your mind. Affirm that you will make it and act accordingly, but affirmation alone is not enough. Action will bring success.

Don't just write what you want to do. Start acting on it as soon as you finish writing to build up energy. This positive vibe is what gives you the inspiration to get out of bed every morning and strive for greatness. There is no way you can give your best and remain the same. Things change for the better. Favor starts locating you. In Sheila's case, she received a salary increase which helped her live a better life. All you need to do is reshape your mind as it is a catalyst for a new outcome. Over time, you will notice a positive change that could significantly shift the direction of your life.

With an optimistic outlook, it's easier to abide by your principles even when things are not going as expected. Sheila was sure she would find someone who truly loved her; that's why she didn't force Phil to stay. She ultimately found happiness. Stop forcing people or things to go the way you want. Just do your part and everything else will fall into place. Focus on maintaining a positive outlook because that's what will help you override challenges and get past obstacles. Every day, remind yourself of what you want to achieve. That will be the force that drives you towards accomplishment. We are re-wiring our brains not just for the journey but to have success along the way.

Below are some ways you can prepare for a successful fitness journey:

- Embrace a growth mindset. Your success will be determined by how you approach obstacles. If you're feeling stuck in the past, it's time to reject that way of thinking that lies to you and develop a winning outlook. Visualize yourself losing the desired weight or being in better shape. Invest time in nurturing a new way of thinking, which makes you see the possibility of improvement in the future. A positive change will set the pace for success.
- Plan and Prepare. It's important to plan and prepare as much as possible before starting over. This will enable you to gain more self-confidence, and by planning and preparing, you will have more control of things.

- Develop a healthy routine before embarking on your fitness journey. A pre-workout routine like meditation, mindfulness or stretching can help you finish your session without feeling exhausted. You might have to make some adjustments, and adapting to change could take time. Do things in the order of their importance. It may not be easy at first, but you'll enjoy the results. You'll be able to get more things done and still find time to focus on personal growth.
- Check your self-talk. The conversations you have with yourself directly reflect your mindset. If you keep telling yourself you're not good enough to achieve your goals, your thoughts will create your reality, and this can prevent you from living a victorious life. To improve your disposition, change your negative self-talk and transform it into something positive.
- Determine that fitness will be a lifestyle and act accordingly. Select what you want to achieve and ask yourself: "Which mindset do I need to embrace to achieve this outcome?" For example, if you want to remain strong and fit, you need to think and talk like this: "I love taking care of my body, nourishing it with quality foods and exercising regularly". It's your goal to

be healthy and fit, so act as if you already have the mind of a healthy and fit person. This helps your brain to adopt a new way of thinking. What follows is making it a reality by acting.

- Surround yourself with people that have your desired mental toughness. Start spending time with people who are very successful and seem to have consistency in doing things successfully. It is easy to adopt a new approach when you see that it is already working for other people. Learn how they think and observe their daily habits to develop the right behavior.
- Practice mental conditioning to strengthen your mettle. Integrate powerful thoughts into your day. These tendencies will facilitate your mindset change and complement your thinking with action. If you are transitioning from a "fixed" to "growth" mentality, schedule time for learning and start writing your lessons and accomplishments every day. In doing so, you will be better equipped to handle adversity and not quit.
- Get out of your comfort zone. Whenever you put yourself in challenging situations, you feel compelled to rise to the occasion and transform. It becomes a necessity if you really want to move forward. Stop and

ask yourself, "What situations can I put myself in that will require me to act with a different way?" When you're in a challenging situation, you're training yourself to try new things that ultimately make you better. You might need to go the extra mile (sometimes literally) so that you can experience growth. Fitness is a step by step journey that will at times be painful, but the reward that comes eventually is worth your perseverance. You have permission to change.

- Ditch the perfection. You may not get where you want the first time you try. Don't let that discourage you. If you set the bar too high, you will feel disappointed the moment you fail to reach your target. Give yourself time and keep on finding inspiration to maintain progress. Pursue excellence instead of perfection.
- Don't worry about what others think. To reduce pressure, focus on your current performance, not what everybody else is expecting. Remember, you're not the only one who is embarking on a new journey. People have started from the ground and slowly worked their way up. You can do it too…perhaps even better!
- Keep track of what you want to accomplish. Check your to-do list and follow up on the things you're supposed

to do by the end of the day, week, or month. Try writing your goals down on paper so that they will be easy to remember. Keep on revisiting to stay on track.

Mental conditioning is something you must do daily if you want an unstoppable belief. I encourage you to make a weekly mindset exercise calendar. Below is one that I use.

Sunday	Monday	Tuesday	Wednesday	Thursday	Friday	Saturday
Visualize a great week	Believe that you add value	Throw away negative thoughts	Stay committed to your goals	Focus on helping more people	Finish strong and expect to win	Reflect and pat yourself on the back

If you implement these key strategies, you are well on your way to a stronger mind that will produce great results. Ponder these words by Og Mandino to further your mental conditioning growth.

"I will act now. I will act now. I will act now. Henceforth, I will repeat these words each hour, each day, every day, until the words become as much a habit as my breathing and the action of blinking my eyelids. With these words, I can condition my mind to perform every action necessary for my success. I will act now. I will repeat these words again and again and again. More importantly, I will walk, where failures fear to walk. I will work when failures seek rest. I will act now, for it is all I have. Tomorrow is the day reserved for the labor of the lazy. I am not lazy. Tomorrow is the day, when the failure will succeed. I am not a failure. I will act now. Success will not wait. If I delay, success will become wed to another, and lost to me forever.

This is the time.

This is the place.

I am the person".

Action steps:

1. Develop a growth thought process.
2. Create a weekly mindset exercise calendar.
3. Learn to appreciate the journey.
4. Act daily.

JOURNEY THREE:

HAVE AN EARTH-SHAKING REASON THAT WILL KEEP YOU FOCUSED

I remember being asked to speak at a Christmas party for a company, and the CEO wanted a big picture message, yet something that would pull on the heart string of each employee. After giving it some thought, I settled on the title You Incorporated, "It's about you, but not only about you" was the driving point for my talk that evening. This message is very applicable to your fitness as well. You are not keeping fit just to fulfill an obligation or impress anyone. You're keeping fit for a reason, and it should be big enough to inspire you every day. Your body is a company, and you must take ownership of it. You will need a big enough and precise enough reason to stick with your fitness, nutrition, and wellness goals. Keep digging until it's big enough. When determining why you should maintain fitness, the physical and psychological benefits come to mind first, but the reason you keep going should be personal to you. Do you want to have better cardiovascular health? Is a healthy weight important to you? Are you determined to alleviate the effects of anxiety and depression? Whatever the reason is, let it be the driving force that prevents you from quitting.

Looking at Sheila's story, the desire to succeed in life became her main reason for creating a realistic fitness routine. She knew that if she could take care of herself, her overall wellness would improve, and she would be able to continue with her career so that she could raise her son comfortably. At the back of her mind, Sheila felt that neglecting her well-being would negatively affect other areas of her life. This is very true. You need to be physically, mentally, emotionally and spiritually healthy if you want to succeed. If you focus on one or two areas and neglect the others, you are bound to fail at some point. All-round empowerment is essential. It is a prerequisite for happiness and success.

Jack's story clearly illustrates how someone can succeed in one area and fail in another. When he started out in his career, he had the zeal and energy that impressed his boss and led to a permanent position. But as time went by, Jack would completely abandon his fitness. Eventually, his career would suffer. Fatigue and depression put him at risk of losing his job and if he hadn't acted in time, he would have to deal with the consequences of wrong choices. Jack paused for a moment and asked himself why staying fit was important. The benefits were far-reaching. If he got back on track and overcame the obstacles, he would keep his job, be happy again and start a family. His future would be secure only if he stayed fit. Those three reasons were prominent enough to make Jack change his manner of living. Every morning when he woke up, he would think about his future and fulfill the promise to never quit. This is what ultimately brought happiness and success to his life. Shelia's story should help you dig deep to find your real "why". As a fitness professional, I've consulted thousands of clients over my twenty years of helping people get and stay fit. One thing I know for sure, the first response to the question, "why do you want to achieve this particular aspiration?" is never the true reason. I want to uncover the ugly truth about why a person wants to change.

Here's what you must understand, the real reason is usually deeply hidden and masked with an answer like "1 want to lose weight."

While this may have some merit to what you want to achieve, it's not going to shake the foundation of the earth when obstacles come your way. I have found some powerful reasons from various clients that I'll share to give you a better understanding of finding your weapon.

"I want to lose weight because my husband is no longer attracted to me."

"I'm afraid of dying prematurely and having another man raise my kids."

"I hate the way my body looks. I have no confidence."

"I want to be a better parent to my kids, so I need to get healthy."

"My sex drive has vanished, and I'm embarrassed."

Ok, now we are getting somewhere and discovering deep and personal reasons that can propel an individual to not quit. It's about you, but not only about you. Are you searching your closet (your inner being) for why you want to get or stay fit?

Do you feel a rumble from the ground? Hopeful you do.

Jack and Shelia both had reasons; they encountered challenges and setbacks, they both had to monitor their situation and make the needed adjustments. One found success and lost his health and got it back. The other was hurting and fearful of not succeeding in life, so she neglected her well-being. Eventually, she regained her fitness and found happiness. This is why fitness is a tool or weapon for overcoming. Not losing sight of a 6 pack abs, losing weight, or running your first marathon, I'm just highlighting that fitness is and should be utilized to make you better. No longer is physical fitness a chore, but a resource.

The importance of having a reason to stay fit is that you don't lose your focus, even after you've gone through the worst. The possibility that everything will get better in the coming days keeps you focused and determined. What you're doing now can change your future and make it brighter. If you're consistently working your way up and maintaining a movement-based lifestyle, you will soon enjoy good results. While you have an earth-shaking reason to keep fit, you should integrate consistency, perseverance, and patience. All these make up a perfect recipe for winning. If you come across challenges along the way, you will have developed resilience that enables you to get back up and continue with your journey.

Let’s see what we can learn from Tim’s story that can help us continue to grow. By most standards, collegiate and pro athletes are in superb shape as the demands of their sport calls for such. Once the playing days have ended, life can be very hard on former athletes. Weight gain, depression, and lack of purpose are just a few challenges many of them face. Tim played college baseball and was a fine shortstop and could field the position with the best of them, and he possessed the hitting prowess to be drafted in the 2nd round of the MLB draft his junior year. After a 4-year stint in the minor leagues and a not so promising future in the big leagues, Tim elected to retire from baseball and start his career in sales. After working for several years, Tim really missed baseball, but what he missed most was the discipline of training and working out to stay in peak shape.

In years, a once lean, athletic Tim had put on 40lbs since his playing days. Math tells us that's a little over 13lbs per year and slightly above 1lb (0.45 kg) per month. Either way, it wasn't good for Tim's mental or physical well-being. Most of his weight gain was belly fat, which is always an ever-increasing danger for heart disease. After several years on his job with lackluster sales numbers, Tim was under heavy stress to perform. This, coupled with his already sedentary way of living, did not bode well for Tim's health and happiness.

One day, Tim hopped on the device that usually gives a 3-digit number that we are supposed to understand, and he noticed he'd lost 11lbs doing absolutely nothing. This got Tim excited, even though he was still sluggish and had low energy. As a former athlete, he knew how to push through tough days. Soon Tim was down 18lbs with no effort or change in nutrition or exercise. This got him a little concerned, so on his next doctor visit, he mentioned the unexplained weight loss to his primary doctor. After some extensive blood work, Tim heard the jaw-dropping "C" word from his doctor, "You have cancer". As a former baseball player, Tim knows life is much like the game he played, filled with ups and downs, as well as opportunities for redemption. He was still young with so much life ahead of him, and Tim wanted to fight. He gathered the information from doctors about his condition and treatment plan, as well as consulted the right team of people to help him make immediate life changes. Was he still emotional? Sure! Was he ready for action? Undoubtedly! His nutritionist worked to create an anti-inflammatory meal plan for Tim that he followed consistently. He created a functional home gym thanks to a fitness trainer that would eliminate excuses not to workout. Tim also got back to prayer and meditation, a principle he once participated in daily. He now has a big reason to make changes and stay true to a better lifestyle. While Tim didn't want a cancer diagnosis to be the reason to start working out and eating more nourishing meals, it became his why. He took his recommended treatments for his cancer, started working out 3-4 days per week, added a daily dose of prayer/meditation, and would eventually beat cancer. This is being down 2 runs in the bottom of the 9th inning with a chance to win the game. Tim stepped up to the plate and acted with his well-being, but it's worth asking, "What caused Tim to gain 40lbs of unwanted weight?" In his words, "I've struggled with self-esteem issues since I was a kid and after baseball, I just didn't feel all that valuable, so I ate myself miserable." Occasionally, the root cause is external and often, it's internal. We must deal with what causes us to not start or abandon what we've started. Tim found his earth-shaking reason and hopefully, you have as well. Don't wait until trouble arrives before you decide to act. Keep going!

To not quit and to succeed, your plan requires synergy or a combination of things working well together for a winning outcome.

Here are ways to stay focused while pursuing fitness:

- Have set goals. Don't just say, "I want to lose weight." Be more specific and say, "I want to lose 20 pounds (9.07 kg) this year because…." Your fitness mark should have a determined timeframe so that you can easily keep track of your progress.

- Be realistic. Don't expect to see instant results as soon as you begin your journey. Have objectives that align with the effort and commitment that you can dedicate to them. While you work to see results, ensure you have the resources necessary to achieve your goals.

- Set reminders. Put sticky notes where you will see them constantly. They will remind you of the benefits of exercise and sticking to your targets.

- Schedule your workout. Allocate time for working out on your calendar, just as you would a doctor's appointment or work. Fitness is that important. For more convenience, you can use your phone to set an alarm when it's nearly time to start.

- Think about the challenges. Consider what might get in the way of you successfully finishing a workout session. Then think of a strategy to overcome these obstacles. For example, if you have kids that need supervision and there is no one else to watch them, get a stroller or bike for them, so they can join you.
- Get a fitness partner. If you feel you might not stick to your fitness routine, find someone who will help you be accountable for your actions.
- Consider joining a social networking site or online community with fitness trainers and nutrition experts and support from other people who are aiming to maintain healthy eating and exercise routines. People who get this kind of support are proven to reach their fitness goals compared to those who do it alone. Additionally, requesting your workplace to offer on-site fitness, yoga, or Pilates classes will also support your ambition to embrace a fit life.
- Incorporate fun and variety. Naturally, human beings need change and variety to stay motivated. We also need

to have fun even when we're working hard. So, why not do both? It could be a toning and Zumba class that changes choreography every week, or a weekly jog that takes you to new places every time. Whatever you choose to do, let your exercise routine revolve around a variety of exercise methods. Make sure you include activities you truly enjoy and are excited about doing. Such activities can even make you forget you're working out — like dancing or playing sports with family and friends.

- Listen to your inner voice when choosing the best workout for yourself. Integrating variety in your routine challenges your body in unique ways, which may introduce you to new muscle groups you didn't know you had. Don't be afraid to try out activities that challenge you positively. They actually encourage growth. Ta'i chi and yoga, for example, have multiple benefits such as mental therapy and physical activity. You can also try a personalized exercise prescription designed by a fitness professional.

- Make it a habit. Maintaining a frequency in your routine will contribute to faster growth and improvement. When you plan for physical activity and engage in it regularly, you will create a sustainable behavior that becomes so innate you won't miss a session.

- Have a killer playlist that can motivate you while you work out.
- Think of a morning workout to set your day in the right direction. For example, exercising can significantly impact your mental health. It can help you handle difficult situations better. Working out can also be a way of releasing energy and frustration. Training in the morning can start off your day in the right direction by giving you sustained energy and focus.
- Reward yourself. A tangible reward is powerful because your brain becomes more aware of it and gets the conviction that consistency is worthwhile. Creating a neurological habit loop which involves a cue to trigger the behavior (like putting on your workout attire), the routine (finishing an aerobic exercise) and the reward. If you keep rewarding yourself, it's more likely that the routine will become a habit. As you maintain consistency, the motivation will become intrinsic as your brain begins to associate physical activity with the surge of endorphins (the feel-good chemicals released in

the brain responsible for that astonishing feeling you get after a workout session.) After you train your brain to recognize that the workout itself is the reward, you will probably not need another reward.

- Consider working out as your "you" time. Think of the activities you participate in as your mental vacation or a chance to get a break and step back from a busy day. Turn exercise into a treat rather than a chore. This will make you stay present and focus on the workout. You won't be counting down the minutes left.
- Personalize your workouts to fit your mood. For example, if you feel like you've spent too much time indoors, you might need to do cardio or go for an outdoor run. If you don't have much energy, focus on relaxing activities like stretching and foam rolling. Do anything that will help improve your mood. Personalized activities are therapeutic, relaxing and motivating.
- Consult a trainer. A professional fitness trainer will help you choose the right exercises based on your goals, needs, likes, and fitness level. A competent fitness coach will educate and inspire you to be better.

- Keep in mind, having an earth-shaking reason for accomplishing any life desire leads to taking consistent action.

Action steps:

1. Find your earth-shaking reason why.
2. Write it down and see it daily.
3. Get help from a professional if needed.
4. Use fitness as a resource.

"Acting is the only thing that really works. Ideally, you want a good process that will maximize your progress."

The Workout

JOURNEY FOUR:

BREAK DOWN YOUR GOALS

At this stage of life or at least this point in reading, you should know more about yourself, working on improving your mindset, and have found a reason to keep going. It's the building blocks that create the height in your journey. You need ambition, you need purpose, you need a plan, and you need a process. A former baseball coach threw it to me this way, Proper Preparation Prevents Piss Poor Performance or the 6 "P's" as he coined it. What are we preparing for? To win is my answer, and hopefully, it's a part of your answer as well. For discovery, let's look at weight loss, since it is a confusing and unmuted subject. Shelia, Jack, and Tim all lost some weight. Shelia, after having a baby, Jack lost some pounds after realizing he was no longer lean and fit. Or did they? What they really did was mobilize fat and move it to the oven to be burned as fuel. Are you ready to sign up? Of course, there's no Fat Mobilization Transportation companies out there, but the process is real. Let's take a look at the psychological and physiological goal of losing 10lbs of fat, so you can be more attractive to your partner and enjoy better a sex life.

1. You have a specific goal, a big enough reason, you have visualized your success, and your mind is ripe for the journey.
2. You know through basic physiology, the body can't shed more than 1-2 lbs of fat each week without some extreme measure. (I know your cousin told you she lost 10 pounds (4.54 kg) in two days on the whatchamacallit diet).
3. You set a 4-8 week time frame to achieve the desired results with the right approach and strategy for training, nutrition, and recovery.
4. You understand that body composition will always be superior over the scale that often defines success.
5. With concern for your mind (the driver), your movement (the ride or run), your muscle (the delivery location), and your meals (the delivery), you are ready for the challenge.
6. You are aware there is no escape route, so you stay the course and make needed changes until the mission has been accomplished.

Is it really that simple? Yes it is, but unfortunately, the murky waters of misinformation produce a feeling of drowning and often, our wellness becomes abandoned. The good news is that won't be you because you know what you want, and you know there are many measurable points along the way.

The Way Maker

To achieve what you want, you should be intentional, especially regarding your fitness. By doing so, it will give you more clarity about the milestones you need to reach next. You won't feel overwhelmed because there's a long way to go. Instead, you'll focus better on your short-term steps. Once you start, find different ways to measure progress, i.e., more energy, lower blood pressure, dropping two dress sizes and so on. Be sure to start with small improvements. Over time and with consistency, this process will lead to accomplishing bigger gains.

Why It's Important to Set Fitness Targets

Before you begin the process of setting and trying to achieve fitness and health goals, it's good to understand why doing so is important. This will help maintain focus because you already know the benefits you'll reap afterwards. It's a fact that you'll see more and better results when you start with an achievable, clearly defined objective rather than working out with no vision.

Make Change Seem More Reachable

Many people hesitate to participate in fitness training because making significant changes seems impossible. For instance, if you've been struggling with weight issues, it can take a lot of willpower and courage to hit the gym. You have obviously wanted to lose weight for a long time, but starting the journey felt like trying to climb an insurmountable mountain. Don't let that discourage you. Begin by setting small, actionable goals, and you will see how possible change is. You can't just start climbing a mountain. You first walk along a rough road, then you advance to numerous hills, one by one and as you progress, the top of the mountain is within reach.

Spark Your Motivation

One of the most common challenges you will face is staying motivated. But if you have goals all drawn up, you have something to refer to repeatedly, and it will act as a source of motivation. Treasure your goal. Whether it's a certain weight loss or being able to finish an aerobic session without giving up halfway through it, this will serve as your spark for ongoing improvement. Keep pushing!

Effort Ensure Progress

You have deadlines to meet; therefore, you will begin to see the progress you're making as a result of persistent effort. If you want to lose a certain number of pounds in a year, for instance, you can measure that. You'll notice that the effort you're putting in and the planning you are doing is actually paying off, and that will give you more motivation to continue.

You Can Make Workouts Efficient

When you have a worthwhile reason to exercise, every workout session will be more goal-oriented than it would be without a vision. Without something concrete to work towards, you can't properly focus on reaching a milestone. With the right mindset, you'll make the most of your time by concentrating on exactly what you want to achieve and the strategies that will bring results.

Without Vision, It Will Be Hard to Succeed

When you don't have firm goals set up, ongoing success becomes more difficult to achieve. You may lose a few pounds, and you'll probably become more energetic, but will you stick with it? Only you can truly answer that. Being definitive gives you an idea of the direction you should take to fully get the most out of your workout routine. You will not be swayed by distraction or discouragement along the way because you've made up your mind to reach a particular milestone within a certain period of time.

Fitness marks are important in many other ways. They make us become accountable, redefine our perspective of what's possible, and inspire us to navigate through temporary discomfort for longer-lasting changes. When a goal is thoughtful and well-structured, it can give you the extra incentive to keep going when you don't seem to have enough motivation or when life gets in the way.

Focus on one goal at a time. When setting a fitness goal, one of the biggest mistakes people make is trying to do too much at one time. Maybe you want to hit the gym four times a week, cut out excess sugar, eat healthy meals and get enough rest. When there are so many things to achieve, it's easy to get anxious, and if you fail to do one thing, you will feel like a failure. This can result in negative self-talk that reduces your chances of achieving forward progress.

Instead of overloading yourself, pick one thing you want to do, like working out or changing your diet. Then direct all your efforts into achieving that before venturing into the next one.

Customize your approach. It can be easy to scroll through social media and feel inspired by images of others who are perfectly fit. Everyone has their journey. Accept where you are and plan the direction you want to go with your fitness. Your goal should be your own, something that you are personally excited about and realistically able to reach.

What You Want Must Be Specific, Measurable and Time-bound.

Having a measurable goal allows you to assess your progress and the more absolute your goal is, the clearer the path to achieving it becomes. A desire to be stronger, for example, is a great place to start, but it should have a special meaning to you. Perhaps you want to increase your endurance, or you want to build up muscle strength. Be specific about what you'd like to gain in the end. Deciding to increase the number of push-ups you can do makes the goal measurable, and planning to be able to do 20 push-ups in one set makes it individual. Additionally, the goal should be time-bound because this helps you focus your efforts, develop a more structured plan for successfully achieving the goal, and creates a sense of accountability that can compel you to complete your workouts.

A great way to make progress is through the SMART method, which helps you make sure your goal is specific, measurable, attainable, relevant, and timely.

Be decisive — clearly define your goal.

Effective goal setting is not about writing a vague idea of what you want to achieve.

Remember that when you have a clear-cut goal, it's easier to know if you have reached it and to map out the steps you need to take to accomplish it. Let's look at this. The goal "I want to get fit" is not specific enough. What's your definition of fit? How will you be able to determine if you are fit? This vague goal doesn't give you a clear direction. When setting a goal, thinking about the "who, what, when, where, why, and how" of your desired outcome can help. You should clearly describe what you are trying to achieve.

An example of an exact fitness goal is: "I want to be able to jog three miles without stopping". Trying to reach this particular goal means you are working towards getting your cardiovascular system fitter and stronger. It also makes you focus on your progress, which makes it easier to work towards improvement.

Hopefully, you are pushing in the right direction. Do you see signs of an expected outcome? If you can track your results against an identified point of reference, it means if you are getting closer to achieving them! This can play an important role in motivating you to continue working towards the mark.

Some examples of measurable fitness goals are:

- Achieve a certain number of repetitions of an exercise, for example, 20 push-ups.
- Run a set distance (3 miles (ca. 5 km)).
- Lift a certain amount of weight (Bench press 250lbs).

It is important to be able to measure and track your goal uniquely. By specifying how often you want to exercise, you can measure your progress by keeping track of how much you can successfully complete over time.

Your goals should be achievable. Even though all goals should be challenging, they must become achievable. This does not mean that you should not go ahead and set big goals for yourself. What you need to do is break those big goals down into smaller, achievable goals that lead towards the bigger goal.

Let's consider the goal of running a marathon. If you are a beginner, an achievable version of this goal might be to aim to run a 5k in three months. Then, you can set a goal of a 10k distance for your next progression, and eventually running towards the objective of 26.2 miles (42.16 km). Each step along the way is broken down and achieved. This is your fitness journey, so approach it that way.

You need to set marks that you can realistically do the work to achieve, considering your resources, current fitness level, and the time you are available.

Think about why you want to achieve a particular goal — will it improve your quality of life? Maybe you want to feel stronger and healthier so that you can be more active. This is a meaningful goal and because it motivates you, there's a greater likelihood you will be committed to working towards it.

Another example — if you decide to complete five evening workouts at the gym every week when it doesn't suit your lifestyle (for example, if you have a young family or a tight work schedule), then this might not be a relevant or realistic goal for you. Aim to set your goals high, but make sure they suit your current situation.

Goals should be time-specific. Setting a start time and deadline for your goal matters a lot. It allows you to work out a plan to achieve the goal by breaking it into daily actions and smaller milestones.

If you set yourself a realistic time frame, it will be easier to prepare and schedule the time you'll need to set aside towards achieving your goal, and you're more likely to be motivated to work towards a deadline.

Regularly review your progress. Every goal requires you to keep track of your progress. You may need to be flexible. It's advisable to revise your plans if you encounter a fitness setback so that other areas of your life will not be compromised. Find a way to track your fitness so that you can observe your progress and maintain momentum as you keep working towards your goal. If you need to have regular rewards and reminders, try using a fitness tracker to record workouts and set your daily movement goals.

Another meaningful way to document your progress over time is to keep a journal to record whether you have achieved the smaller goals and actions that are part of your plan to achieve your bigger ones.

Write the reasons for selecting that goal and the details of the aspiration. Once you know exactly what your new fitness objective is, you can make time for exercise and draw up a game plan to achieve it.

When setting your SMART goals, they must be your personal goals and are meaningful and relevant to you. Don't compare what you want to accomplish to that of other people because everyone is on a personal journey with unique milestones and challenges.

A lot of work goes into setting and working towards a goal, but once you've done it once and achieved your goal, it'll be easier to set the next goal.

As you begin, set the bar high, but make sure the progressions are reachable. If a goal is attainable, it might seem relatively easy or within reach. If you think it's easy, you have likely already worked through any mental obstacles that could hinder your progress. Looking at it based on a confidence scale. You should score 9 out of 10 when it comes to your belief that you'll actually achieve your goal. The less confident you are, the less likely you will stick to the steps needed to make it happen. Furthermore, attainable goals help ensure that you start out with the most valuable wins. The more success you have in your fitness journey, the more you will be consistent. Succeeding early on is especially important as it builds confidence that can lead to long-term results. When Jack decided to get his fitness back, he could complete the small milestones he laid out for himself. This gave him more confidence and a desire to move forward.

Next, patience is essential. We all want instant gratification, but it's important to be realistic with the time frame you develop for achieving your goal. Lasting changes take some time.

Keep in mind that you will not make a complete turnaround in one week. Instead, pick a focused objective that can be achieved over the course of several months or even a year. A long-term mentality will help you see your goal as a permanent change rather than a quick fix, and you'll be much more likely to stick to it.

Know what's driving your purpose. Sometimes fitness determination can be driven by insecurities or body image issues. Understanding this can help you in many ways. It's important to address any underlying problems instead of assuming achieving your goal will resolve them.

Depending on what you are trying to accomplish, a goal can trigger many emotions. If thinking about your goal brings anxiety or triggers past mental struggles, talk with a mental health professional before beginning your journey.

Be flexible in your definition of success. While it is important to make your goal relevant, it's similarly significant to give yourself permission to modify it as you progress with your fitness journey. For instance, you set a goal of losing 20lbs, but you only lost 10lbs while gaining more energy. That is an achievement, so view it that way.

If your roadmap to success is rigid, it provides an easy pathway to quit, especially when it comes to fitness. Set goals you think you can achieve, and then modify them as you understand more about what you are capable of doing. Don't feel guilty if you have to move the goalposts as you get more comfortable with your body's capabilities.

Prioritize small wins in the beginning. It's all about those little achievements. Celebrate being able to run one mile. It's encouraging to be able to reward yourself mentally. Having to wait for too long to feel like you've accomplished anything can dampen your motivation and pull you off track entirely.

As you start out, it's good to set micro-goals that can be achieved every two to three weeks. That amount of time can help you determine if your big goal is realistic and provide the chance to scale things back if necessary.

Seek a professional's input. If you're having a hard time assessing your current fitness level, determining what would be a realistic goal, or just feeling overwhelmed about the process, it can be helpful to consult an expert, like a certified personal trainer. A professional can help give you guidance on how realistic your goal is and help you set markers along the way, so you can check in and confirm you are on the right track as time goes by.

They will ask you about various factors influencing your lifestyle, including your prior history with fitness (e.g., Have you trained before? Are you a former athlete? Do you have experience lifting weights?), your nutrition, work and social history (e.g., Do you have a demanding high-stress job? Do you go out frequently? Etc.). These questions are to understand. Once the trainer understands your life, they can create a program around what works for you.

In addition, a trainer will conduct several athletic tests—like endurance tests and strength tests—to assess your baseline level of fitness. You can ask yourself these questions and conduct fitness tests on yourself, but if you're new to fitness, it may be helpful to get an expert's input.

Always be honest about your prior and current habits. Asking yourself the tough questions can help you honestly evaluate what's most appropriate for you. In case you are someone who in the past crushed several fitness goals and just wants to take it to the next level, you could likely handle a more complex goal, like running a long-distance race at a certain pace.

But if you're new to fitness, you will need to focus on more simple behavior modifications, like going to the gym a certain number of days a week.

You have to be realistic with what you are currently doing if you want to see remarkable progress. If your routine doesn't involve any kind of exercise, it will be unreasonable to suddenly get yourself to the gym five days a week. Be practical and reasonable as you start.

Furthermore, it's helpful to be aware of what has stopped you from achieving goals in the past. If you always have a hard time getting up in the morning, for example, sign up for evening workout classes rather than aiming for those 6 a.m. sessions. Being honest with yourself will help you recognize and get rid of barriers before you get started.

Get a support system. When thinking about your goal, you should also think about who's in your life could encourage, motivate, and hold you accountable for it. Then consult them whenever you need support. If the people you spend the most time with are supportive of your goals, it will make a significant difference.

Avoid These Common Mistakes When Setting Goals

Now you know that setting goals needs much more consideration than many people imagine. Anyone can set a goal in seconds, but to do it right takes thought and planning. Successful goal setting also requires avoiding some mistakes. Learn from the mistakes of others and avoid these common mistakes:

- Setting negative goals. Don't allow yourself to set goals like 'not being fat' or 'never eating junk food again.' Success is more achievable with positive goals like having a healthy weight or eating more vegetables.
- Being hesitant to adjust goals as needed. Adjustment doesn't mean you're failing. Always be prepared to alter goals if you notice they are not realistic or need more time.
- Failing to keep track of progress. Put your goals in writing, and then keep record of their progress. When you measure and record progress, you get to see the benefits of your efforts, and this gives you the will to keep on growing.
- Punishing failures. Avoid the idea of failure altogether, and even if you fail, don't punish yourself. Instead, identify where you went wrong and what you can do differently to ensure improvement.
- Failing to reward achievements. Rewards can be helpful and motivating. Acknowledge each small win and each bit of progress recorded.

- Focusing on perfection. This can hurt your fitness motivation. Therefore, expecting it sets even the most motivated person up for failure. Focus on progress and growth.

Goals must be meaningful. Have a simple plan of action to achieve them. There needs to be an emotional attachment, which is why you must carefully set your own. Setting goals is the first step towards making positive changes that last.

Try our goal setting rating below to get instant feedback.

Goal Setting Questionnaire

DEGREE OF SATISFACTION with Current Level of Fitness.

Check the best number of each aspect of your current fitness level using the scale:

4 = very satisfied 3 = satisfied 2 = dissatisfied 1 = very dissatisfied

4

3

2

1

Areas to rate

*CARDIOVASCULAR ENDURANCE

*MUSCULAR STRENGTH AND ENDURANCE

*FLEXIBILITY OF HAMSTRINGS AND LOW BACK

*AMOUNT OF ENERGY

*ABILITY TO COPE WITH TENSION AND STRESS

*ABILITY TO RELAX

*ABILITY TO GET A GOOD NIGHT'S REST

*LOW BACK FUNCTION

*PHYSICAL APPEARANCE/BODY WEIGHT

AREAS OF IMPROVEMENT

Take a few moments to think about the areas of your life which you feel need improvement. Briefly list areas of improvement below:

1. Risk of a Health Problem:
2. Specific Physical Problem:
3. Appearance of a Particular Part of Body:
4. Ability to participate in a Particular Sport OR Daily Function:

5. Other:

By taking the time to partake in the goal setting questionnaire, you are preparing your mind and body for success. Writing well-planned working goals can help you achieve what may seem to be a difficult achievement.

Action Steps:

1. Establish clear and concise goals
2. Measure success in different ways
3. Evaluate your progress and revise the plan if needed.

JOURNEY FIVE:

SIMPLIFY THE PROCESS

Life is complicated enough. You don't have to make it harder as you strive towards fitness. You want to make the process simple so that you can maintain the consistency that will eventually bring results. When the process is simple and favorable, it will be easier to make progress every week. Both Jack and Sheila eventually knew the importance of goal setting, having a process and a strategy to achieve the goals. The most important part of developing a personal plan for fitness is to know your "why." Yes, this is your earth-shaking reason, but it also leads to the approach you will take with your fitness program. If your goal is to be supple and lean, you probably shouldn't be following a bodybuilding program. Be sure to know your why and understand your goals. To understand both strategies is to better know the subject (You).

It all starts with accepting your weaknesses and acknowledging your strengths. Identifying what could disrupt your progress and finding ways to counter it with your strengths will make it effortless to be consistent. For example, Sheila discovered that she was at her weakest when she wasn't busy. She would think about the way Phil had deserted her. This brought a lot of sadness to her heart. But when she kept herself occupied with work responsibilities and her responsibility to take care of her son, she didn't find the time to remember the difficult position Phil had put her in. Her mood improved, and she began looking forward to her workout sessions. She could improve the quality of her life just because she identified her weakness and found an effective way to deal with it.

You, too, can apply the same technique to make your journey simpler — and enjoyable. Anything that's stopping you from giving your best should be resolved before it forces you to quit. Whether it's a personal issue or a problem at work, don't ignore it. Find the help you need so that as you pursue fitness, you will have comfort and peace. Workouts are much more exciting and effective when there are no underlying issues bothering you. Nothing should get in the way of your zeal and ambition.

What to unpack.

Your fitness journey is not designed to be easy, but you can make it easier.

Control Your Stress Level

This is critical. Your ability to manage stress and how you respond to stressful situations is central to your overall wellness.

Nowadays, most of us are busy as we pursue success, and that can lead to chronic stress. When we work for longer hours and sleep less, stress can build up over time. We only realize its effects when our bodies warn us.

A bit of stress is okay. Mild stress motivates us to achieve more, complete tasks and be more productive. Stress helps us meet deadlines and push ourselves to do better even in difficult situations.

But it becomes a problem when it's chronic. Our stress hormones cortisol and adrenaline will certainly to increase in times of short-term stress and then return to normal.

One of the first things you need to do to reduce stress is improving your sleep. While some people can manage off less than 8 hours, it is the quality of sleep that restores us.

Effective steps you can take to promote more, better quality sleep includes:

- Go to bed at the same time every night.
- Turn electronic devices off 1 hour before bed.
- Dim the lights at night.
- Take a warm shower or bath with Epsom salt.
- Drink herbal tea with chamomile or lavender a few hours before sleep.

- Find ways to relax. Meditation, a long bath or taking a five-minute walk outside when you feel stressed out can relax and refresh you.

If stress is a persistent problem for you, I highly recommend you see a mental health professional.

Ditch the All or Nothing Mentality

You have big goals… then you suddenly develop this mentality that it's either you get 100 percent success or nothing at all. That's the wrong perspective, given that you're bound to make some mistakes or even fail at some point. What matters is that you get back up and start over. There should be no consequences for failing to stick to your nutrition program or missing a workout. What counts is what you do consistently.

The trick when you mess up is to experience the disappointment that you didn't stick to your routine for a moment, and then move forward. Don't start believing that you're a loser or a failure or that you've blown it now, so you might as well go back to your old routine. Just make the next best decision and keep going. It's known as the "Day after Perfect".

Every so often, you may not be able to stick to a plan to see results. What will eventually bring results is being consistent over the long term and improving on what you're already doing. Learn from your flaws instead of letting them bring you down. At some point, you will feel like you've not given your best. Be rational. If you missed a workout session yesterday, missing out for the rest of the week will not help, so shake that self-criticism off and get back on track!

Avoid Emotional Eating

Emotional eating is not healthy. Your gym instructor or personal trainer may not be able to completely assist you, so it's best to see a psychotherapist or a psychologist if you're experiencing this problem.

There's nothing wrong with snacking occasionally or enjoying a meal with your family, even when it doesn't fully correspond to your nutrition program. Automatically turning to food as your go-to coping mechanism at the first sign of an uncomfortable feeling can make healthy eating hard.

One way you can take control of this problem is to keep a food journal. Doing this for a week can reveal eating patterns and the things that trigger what you do. Write:

- When you eat.
- What you eat.
- What you were doing when you ate.

- How you felt before and after you ate.

Be honest with yourself. Try to be a keen observer of your behavior. Once you have an idea of what you've been doing, you can get help to find lasting solutions.

Make Plans!

You are bound to see great results when you schedule your workouts and plan out your meals! Most of us don't do this, but it makes a big difference.

If you want to be successful, you need to plan. It's good to get help, but only you know your lifestyle and what you can adhere to consistently.

It's necessary to plan your meals because you need to eat a few times a day, and you need to book your training sessions and write them in your diary so that you don't miss any session. When you don't plan meals, that's when you find yourself ravenous and prone to making the wrong choices. Keep things simple and know yourself.

In case you really don't have time or don't enjoy cooking, healthy food delivery services are cost-effective. They take the thinking out of things.

Pick one or two meals you like and are quick to prepare, and buy your ingredients during the weekends. You can also rotate between a few simple lunches and dinners. Prepare as much as you can on the weekend. Or if you have the time to cook daily, write out a rough plan early enough, so you have an idea of what will be on your diet.

Working out should be like every other commitment in your life. Prioritizing your fitness makes a huge difference in your overall quality of life. Even if your current plan is just walking every day, make sure you plan at the beginning of the week and every evening when you're going to fit it in.

Minimize Eating Out

As much as it's good to eat nutritious food, it's unreasonable to avoid going to meetings or parties just because you want to avoid making a mistake. You shouldn't miss out on interacting with others to reach your fitness goals.

The truth is that it's harder to eat well and stay on track when you eat out often. When you prepare your food, you have complete control over what goes onto your plate and how much you can eat. It's easy to fall short of your nutrition goals at a restaurant or a social function. The tastiest foods are usually high in fat, calories, and salt. Plus, the portion sizes are usually much more than what you need.

The best way to stay on track is to simply eat out less. Don't miss out, but be choosy about when you do. Instead of eating out every day for lunch and grabbing pizza at night when there is nothing else available, pick one or two occasions a week when you will enjoy eating out or when you will attend social events.

When you eat out, the good thing is you're still controlling what you can have.

You can apply some of these simple tricks for keeping on track when you can't prepare your meals:

- Choose a meal rich in veggies (at least half a plate)
- Go for lean protein.
- Eat smaller portions.
- Limit your intake of soft drinks and alcoholic beverages.

Stop Complicating Things

When most people are trying to lose weight, they immediately draw up a meal plan or a new diet, coupled with a rigorous workout routine. This is definitely a big leap from what you're currently used to, and it automatically sets you up for failure.

You may be smart and successful in your career, but when it comes to fitness, you may experience total failure. This often comes when you make your health and fitness journey hard. Just like you're thriving in your career, it will be better if you thrive in fitness. It doesn't matter how much you know about healthy habits and eating well. As long as the process is overwhelming you, you may not be able to make progress.

Most people who are not athletes will enjoy considerable success by keeping things elementary and getting right back to basics. This, for many people, will mean three balanced meals a day, little or no alcohol, and exercising 3-4 times per week. Making these changes can make a big difference and simplify your fitness journey.

Once you follow the basics, you can personalize the rules for even better results.

Don't Always Focus On Numbers.

Do you aim to reach a certain number on the scale or to fit into a certain outfit? As much as this can be motivating, it can also be equally challenging.

Focusing on numbers can be discouraging, whether it's counting calories or checking your weight daily. One day, you might weigh half a pound less and the next day, you might weigh a pound more. Unless you've over-eaten by 3500 calories throughout the day, the likelihood is that you haven't gained a pound of fat; you may have retained water. Remember, your body is 70% water. With that in mind, it is also important to consider the other factors mentioned that can also affect your weight, such as hormone levels, sleep patterns, stress levels, hydration & nutrition.

In simple terms, the number you see on the scale is not always the most reliable source of progress. When you rely on a number, you're subconsciously neglecting the way that you should truly feel because you're convincing yourself you'll be happy if you reach your 'goal weight'. You might find yourself doing it over and over again until it becomes a vicious cycle. It will then be difficult to change your perspective because your mind will already be used to making conclusions from unreliable numbers.

You can track your progress using a better method. For example, use a measuring tape to measure your hips, waist, arms, etc. and write those numbers and then measure again in 3 months or take before and after photos. It will be easier to identify change that way. Many times when we look at ourselves in the mirror, it's hard to notice the minor changes in our bodies, so taking photos to track our progress can be so helpful. You can do so every 1–3 months, and remember to have patience with yourself; results take time. Enjoy the journey and make it a lifestyle change Instead of something temporary. Body composition or body fat is also a more accurate measure of progress if leanness is your goal.

Embrace the Change

Any change in your routine, whether major or minor, will be uncomfortable at first, and it will be challenging. When your heart is not in it long enough, the likelihood of you achieving that goal is low because you haven't developed the habit for it yet. It's the same as losing motivation and eventually giving up.

Many times we are driven by emotion and give ourselves excuses because we're simply not ready for it. If we depend on whether we feel like it, we probably won't get it done. In fact, you won't always have motivation for the task. But if you are consistent, you will find yourself getting it done. It will become an automatic part of your routine like any other successful habit, There will still be days when you don't feel like exercising, push through those days, and watch how strong you become.

You might be asking yourself how you can develop a consistent habit. There are no shortcuts or tricks, but there are 3 steps that you can take:

- Plan: Planning helps you to stay organized and maintain a good schedule, so you can fit your activity of choice into your routine. Your life may get crazy busy at some point and planning your time in advance will be helpful, especially when you want to incorporate a new habit.
- Review: Go through the process of integrating that habit into your routine. Ask yourself, what am I gaining from this new habit, and how will it affect my life? This

will not only revive motivation, but it will also mentally prepare you for what's ahead.

- Act: Act upon what you have planned and reviewed and encourage yourself to fully focus on it without letting distractions get in the way. Whenever you feel like you can't go on, remind yourself of all the benefits you would miss out on if you neglected your fitness.

Prioritize Short-Term Goals

As much as long-term goals are important, it's essential to record your small achievements because it's the accumulation of those small victories that ultimately enable you to reach your future goals. It's easy to get frustrated along the way and fail to notice those small steps that you've taken, but they are there to remind you that you're well on your way to achieving what you have visualized for yourself.

We often overlook or fail to acknowledge the small successes, and then we become hard on ourselves when we don't achieve the long-term goals.

An example of one small goal can be as simple as remembering to drink a glass of water in the morning as soon as you wake up. Write it down and check it off once you've done it. You will feel a sense of accomplishment and feel inspired to continue with the journey.

Improve Your Nutrition

Nutrition is a significant part of everyone's life, regardless of whether you are working towards a fitness goal or not. Food provides us with energy and nutrition to nourish and refuel our bodies.

When considering your fitness goals, the ratio between food and exercise depends on what you want to achieve. If you want to lose weight, it's common to eat in a slight caloric deficit: eating less than what you're burning. If you want to gain weight, then it's common to eat in a caloric surplus… eating more than what you're burning.

Still, it's good to remember nutrition is not the only factor that's important. For example, an athlete might ask why they're not gaining muscle even though their training super hard. It could partly have to do with their nutrition, or it could be because of not having enough rest/sleep or too much stress in their daily lives. You have to consider all these factors. We need food for nourishment and energy, rest for growth and recovery and a relaxed state of mind, so our bodies can run smoothly.

Everyone will give advice on what you should and shouldn't eat. This can confuse you, so let's look at this. Basically, take these 4 things into consideration:

- Eat whole foods instead of processed foods.

- Choose variety; include an array of fruits & vegetables in your diet.
- Make sure to eat a balance of complex carbohydrates, fats, and protein.
- Drink plenty of water!!

Action Steps:

1. Create a simple action plan.
2. Don't take in too much information.
3. Recognize small wins.

The Cool-down

JOURNEY SIX:

RELY ON YOUR ACCOUNTABILITY TEAM

As you begin to wipe the sweat away from your face knowing you've just finished a great workout, a smile graced your face because you know it's a team effort. Maybe some of your team members are with you, or they could be miles away, but you know they are rooting for you to make it. They are your Elmer's (the glue). These are the people who want you to win. They won't let you give excuses for not following your routine and sticking to the goals you've shared. They may seem tough on you sometimes, but they will not let you quit. Your accountability team will ensure that you abide by the rules, even if it means making changes to your schedule, attitude, or outlook.

It's a fact that committing something to paper has a more profound effect than typing it on your phone or a digital calendar. It's better to buy a wall calendar or a day planner or even an empty notebook and start planning what you want each day, week, and month to consist of pertaining to goal achievement. Write your plan on paper, and then it will be easier to stick to because you can see it.

Don't just schedule your workouts — plan your meals to discourage taking the easy way and stalling your progress with fitness because of unwholesome food choices—expect to win. The more you plan, the more you increase your chances of succeeding.

Once you've written your plan on paper, start taking steps to make it a concrete plan. Sign up for your classes, confirm your schedule with your workout partner, or even write about your intentions on social media — these simple and fast steps will help you hold yourself accountable to your plan.

Learn to invest in your fitness. Whether it's renewing your gym membership, working with a fitness trainer, buying new sneakers or getting a high-tech fitness tracker, investing in your goals helps you feel committed to achieving them. You're more likely to go to the gym you're paying for than you are to use that free exercise video on YouTube. This is because you're not losing anything in value when you skip a few days of YouTube sessions. But if you miss out on going to the gym or your sessions with a trainer — you're spending real money, and it's harder to make excuses to skip the investment.

Accountability partners help you bring your ambition to reality. In Jack's case, his wife helped him continue pursuing his fitness goals when he had to juggle between work, family, and self-care. She knew how important it was for him to stay in shape, both mentally and physically, so she was glad to be part of his accountability team. With encouragement from his trainer, friends and colleagues, Jack successfully found a balance in all aspects of his life. Not one area did he neglect. He thrived in his career and family life. Most importantly, he didn't forget to set aside time for his personal well-being.

A strong team that is always supportive helps you create a balance. Work, family, personal and social life needs balance. This way, you can be assured of great progress that will eventually yield success. You can't neglect one area and expect progress. Either you will stall your progress or other areas will be affected as time goes by. That's why you need a team because you can't achieve great things on your own.

Sheila was lucky to have a close friend who understood her and what she was going through. When Sheila told her friend that she would be incorporating a fitness routine into her schedule, she took it upon herself to help her become accountable. She would remind her of upcoming workout sessions and ensure everything in the house was running smoothly so that there would be no reason for Sheila to lag. That support contributed to Sheila's success in getting back her life.

From this, we learn that the people closest to you can be part of your accountability team. They know your weaknesses and your strengths, and they can use this knowledge to help you overcome the obstacles that could prevent you from moving forward. Surround yourself with people who care about you, people who want to see you shine. Your journey will not only be easier, it will also be full of inspiration and support.

There are many benefits of having an accountability partner. First, you'll be able to do new things. Have you been cooking up the same meals on repeat, or doing the same workout over and over? Teaming up could open up a whole new world of inspiration, either online or in person. Create a powerful team and discover fresh perspectives, whether it's for new recipes or tips on healthy living. Through their support, you'll be inspired to become the best version of yourself. The positive effects of accountability teams can extend to social media and online networks. Accountability partner can cheer us along, give advice and motivate us.

A good team will help shift your way of thinking and put you in position to win. The way you think determines your actions. It's important to surround yourself with positive-minded people, and the positivity will rub off on you. Having conversations that encourage behavioral change can help improve your self-worth. It can also change the way you view your goals and intentions.

Having a team won't just motivate you to work out, it will amp up the efficacy of your session. Healthy competition is very effective.

When one person changes their behavior, the surrounding people can change.

Wellness accountability partners help each other set and pursue goals for diet, exercise and overall well-being. The key fact is that knowing someone else is monitoring you and vice versa sparks accountability and makes it more difficult to cheat when it comes to eating better or working out. Knowing that someone else is counting on you does the same. For example, in instances where you might normally let yourself off the hook for missing a workout, if you have planned one with a partner, it's no longer just about you. You know that if you cancel your workout, you're going to let someone else down. The right people should encourage you and create a favorable, fun, and competitive challenge.

Learn new behavioral-change tricks with the right group. Reconnecting with the reason that compels you to embrace change means that when tough times come, you are more likely to stay motivated for the goal.

Understanding why your workouts are important increases your chances of succeeding. You can boost your accountability through goal setting. It is also helpful to understand the purpose behind your goals. Ask yourself why your workouts matter and how they fit into your lifestyle. This will boost your accountability and motivation.

Be sure to eliminate as many barriers as possible. If you elect to join a gym, and it's more than 10 minutes from your home or work, there's a good chance you will not use it consistently. Holding yourself accountable to work out is possible, but it takes some effort and understanding. You can simplify the process by not allowing anything or anyone between you and your next workout. It might be something simple like laying out your clothes the night before, so you don't have to spend a lot of time before getting to your workout. Do what you can to increase your chances of being present when you need to.

You can improve your accountability level by:

1) Making a schedule.

Review your week and find days and times when you're free to workout. Aim to keep a regular schedule. But if that isn't possible, set your schedule in advance for each individual week.

2) Signing up for regular fitness classes, training programs, or hiring a personal trainer.

Besides knowing you have something scheduled, with organized workouts, there are people waiting for you to be present. If you have trouble sticking to plans, start with attending regular fitness classes. If you discover your attendance is intermittent, register for a one-to-two month training program. And in case you need more accountability, hire a personal trainer. You probably won't cancel on your trainer knowing they are waiting for you and that you might be charged for that session.

There are some simple techniques that you can use that will help you to stay accountable while at the same time working with your accountability partner, who will use these tools to monitor over and verify your progress:

- Start a fitness journal and record your successes.
- Have a food diary to record when and what you are eating.
- Create a rewards program that lets you reward yourself positively.

Being an accountability partner doesn't always mean scheduling workouts together. We all need different types of accountability depending on where we are less responsible. It could be staying active or abiding by portion control at mealtime.

When choosing a fitness partner, you don't have to schedule similar workouts. You can keep track of each other's progress by checking in at least once daily to share whether you're eating healthy, have done a workout, or have practiced self-care. If your character traits and fitness goals overlap, that's an added advantage. Although it makes sense if your goals and your partner's goals align, experts advise that you probably should not be too similar in terms of where you are on the fitness map. Wherever you are now does not have to be similar for you to become accountability partners.

It's advisable to look for someone who has already achieved a greater level of fitness than you, even if they are still on the journey to bigger achievements. A person who has gone through it, who understands the process of adjusting to change and getting in shape, will better understand the ups and downs you're going through.

Look for someone you can trust, someone who will show up. That person should also be able to count on you to do the same. Your accountability partner should give you the right combination of support and tough love. It's not as easy as it sounds. You're teaming up to support each other, not to judge each other's mistakes. The process is all about support, love, and some tough love along the way. Find people who need your help just as you need theirs and with whom you genuinely enjoy spending time, even if it's virtual.

If you thrive in a team setting, it is okay to add more than one person as an accountability partner: The bigger your team is, the more fun you're likely to have. There is also encouragement in numbers; if one person quits, you'll still have other people to count on.

Consider teamwork from a fitness perspective. It is okay if the person is in a little better shape than you or that they're helping you along a bit; however, it may be demotivating when the person is far more seasoned and the gap is too big. If you're running two miles, and they are running ten, you might not feel like you're doing anything meaningful.

Find someone you can properly connect with on this journey. Being able to connect means there's a huge emotional benefit. During a workout, more than our pores open up. We find ourselves connecting with our workout partners more intimately than we might if we were just meeting over a drink. Workout partners not only help us get through a challenging workout, they can help us through life challenges as well. A good partnership is one without distractions. Firmly focus on what brought you together!

It's possible to form a beneficial partnership. Whether you choose Zoom workouts, spreadsheets, or any other method, experts agree that there should be some structure to the arrangement and those daily check-ins are essential. Implementing rules to abide by is necessary. Agree on how long the partnership will last, what your goals are, the information you're going to share and how you will check in.

Despite the responsibility to your partner that comes from an accountability agreement, accountability also helps people realize that it's about them and not about the other person. Regardless of how you carry yourself during the process, you're being accountable to yourself. Whether you work out, drink your water and eat right doesn't affect your team. You're the only one who's going to ultimately enjoy great results.

Establish an active partnership with thoughtful acts of support like these:

- Stay in touch. Send reminder texts or emails, prearrange rides to the gym, or offer wake-up calls when needed.
- Be on time.
- Encourage your partner and reinforce their efforts with praise.
- Suggest new ideas and routines to keep things interesting and prevent monotony. Do a little research to get new ideas and activities you can try.
- Remind your partner of their goals and encourage them when the going gets rough.
- Keep tabs on each other through illness, travel, and other routine-breakers. It will make it easier to get back on track.

- Talk about topics other than fitness. The more you care about your partner as a person, the stronger your alliance will be. Do not dwell on negative talk. It drains motivation.
- Avoid creating large teams as it can be hard to schedule workouts with multiple people. Keep your team small to avoid unnecessary inconveniences.

Action Steps:

1. Select an accountability team.
2. Communicate and meet with them regularly.
3. Bring value to your team.

"I'm not a fan of celebrating mediocrity, but I do believe in the acknowledgement of small victories that I know lead to bigger ones. They are worth it."

JOURNEY SEVEN:

CELEBRATE ALONG THE WAY

We've talked about acknowledging small wins and rewarding yourself. This is necessary to maintain motivation so that you can easily make progress. When you pat yourself on the back every time you accomplish something along the way, you build momentum and growth becomes effortless. Rewards encourage you to continue working towards actualizing your dreams.

Setting big, audacious goals is important if you're aiming to fulfill your potential in both fitness and life. The reality check of setting such big goals can be demotivating once you realize just how much work you have ahead of you. Getting to the top will take a lot of patience and resilience. Occasionally, you will fall, but what you do afterwards will determine whether you will win.

The initial excitement you get from dreaming big is often followed by feeling overwhelmed, making you doubt whether you can pursue such a big goal. Occasionally, you may not even know where to start. But when you learn to acknowledge small wins, you will feel the urge to keep going, no matter how long it takes for you to get to where you want to be.

Small milestones are essentially progress points heading to your larger goal. They remind you that your efforts were not in vain. You may not have hit the target, but you've made some progress. That is the first sign that you are on the road to victory.

These small milestones can act as a checklist on your way to bigger goals. Although they may currently seem small, if you achieve enough over time, they will result in significant progress.

This is how you can harness the power of forward movement to achieve any goal, fitness-related or not. As we start our journey, huge ambitious goals motivate us to act. When you decide you want to start cycling or lifting weights, you initially feel a surge of excitement and motivation. That's because you have not started working towards that goal yet.

That motivation can decrease when you realize just how big and overwhelming that goal really is. Depending on where you currently are and how far you have to go, your new ambition implies that you have months, if not years, of hard work ahead of you.

This is where many people get discouraged and give up before they even give themselves a chance to make notable progress. They let the immensity of their goal overwhelm them, and they convince themselves it's pointless to keep trying. Consequently, they end up quitting before they realize how many mountains they have climbed. Getting sidetracked or bored with our goals can sometimes stall progress. We might have written our goals on paper, yet we start to be uncertain when obstacles challenge us. We may even outline how we're going to achieve that goal, but for some reason, we lose interest and hit the wall.

This happens when we become so fixated on future goals that we tend to overlook all the small victories along the way. We become so wrapped up with the ultimate outcome that we never acknowledge all the obstacles that have been conquered along the way. We must get excited about these small wins, or it will cause our journey to become boring.

The fastest way to lose motivation is failure to acknowledge your achievements. When you set out to accomplish something, the path to get there isn't always a fast and smooth ride. You're going to be frustrated and hit the wall sporadically. No one has ever made it without setbacks. In fact, the setbacks shape you to be a better, more successful person. So don't back out when they come!

The tasks you need to complete to get to where you want to be in life may be challenging, and the journey may be daunting, but you must walk in the present. If you keep on moving along without celebrating how far you have already come or never taking time to observe your own personal growth, you are going to miss out on the beauty of celebrating growth. By giving yourself credit for small milestones along the way, you are more likely to want to keep going.

Ways you can celebrate growth include:

- Buying yourself trendy fitness apparel.
- Pumping your fist in the air in a celebratory manner after you reach 10,000 steps.
- Texting a supportive friend or significant other about your progress.
- Putting a checkmark on your calendar each time you complete a workout.

You can also do things that you enjoy. It can be playing games, attending a sporting event, watching a movie, etc. Whatever you do, just ensure that the reward is something that you look forward to doing. When you look forward to something you enjoy, thinking about it improves your energy and motivation levels.

A great way to reward hard work is to give yourself a gift. Depending on the size of your progress, if you think you have done a good job, give yourself a small gift. Similarly, if you have done a superb job and accomplished something bigger, give yourself a bigger reward.

Another good way to celebrate your wins is to involve others. While you celebrate, you want to avoid involving just anyone but someone who supports you and cares about you. That person will be happy for you, and will also encourage you to go further.

Sharing your victories with others is great because it makes you feel more accountable. It is as effective as making a public commitment. When you announce and share your goals with someone else, you are putting yourself on the line.

You may feel a little ridiculous celebrating after your wins and want to avoid this step—don't. As ridiculous as it may feel at the time, adding celebration to your wins will make the entire process of working toward a goal more positive and help you stay motivated even when you are dealing with challenges.

No matter how big your goal, always remember that slow progress is still progress. Keep working on what you want to achieve, and in a while, you will have made so much headway that you will have to reach for even bigger aspirations.

Growth is optional! You have chosen a path which offers a better today and tomorrow.

Be sure to form routines that help you to achieve small wins. For you to have something to celebrate, it is important to intentionally try to get better. This can only be achieved by developing good habits. These are activities which you do without having to think twice. They come naturally to you because you have programmed your mind and body to suit them. That's why you should aim to create a routine that will ensure improvement. You can do this by following a plan that helps you become insanely consistent at completing important daily tasks. Establish them in all areas of your life. The objective is to achieve your fitness goals, and to do so, you must make forward movement.

How to Tell If You are Making Progress in Your Fitness Journey

- Everyday tasks are getting easier for you. Although slimming down is certainly a common motivation behind fitness, the real-world progress you feel can be a much more powerful inspiration to keep going. Notables such as walking up the stairs at work without needing to rest, playing with your kids on the weekends, etc. These are some of the reasons you stay fit and healthy.

- You have achieved a fitness goal. Whether your goal is to do three workouts per week or compete in a fitness event, you have giving yourself the gift of done by achieving the task. Working your way up to bigger goals or participating in more events can be a clearer indication of success. Measure your success!

- You are feeling more energetic. A change in your diet can have major positive results other than losing weight, especially if you have been lacking energy. If you have noticed an improvement in your energy levels throughout the day, this could mean you are successfully balancing your blood sugar levels. This can give your body unlimited energy.

- Your mood has improved. In case you recently started a new fitness routine and are noticing that you feel happier, then that is a pretty good measure of success. We have learned that regular exercise helps increase circulation, core body temperature and release endorphins. These feel-good hormones give you that 'happy' feeling after working out, which helps you control the lows that come when the temperatures reduce and the body wants to go into hibernation mode.

- You are noticing more muscle definition. Even if that number on the scale is the same, you may notice more defined arm muscles or less puffiness in your face, all of which are signs that you are making progress.

- Your endurance is improving. You might notice you can complete your cardio workouts more easily or can add a few more minutes to that run or bike ride. That means you may not only be building muscle, but also improving your cardiovascular endurance.

- You feel stronger. Maybe you are lifting heavier weights at the gym, or carrying groceries feels a little easier than it used to. Take note of your strength gains. If it was initially hard to even get through a workout session, but now you feel energized afterwards, then you are doing great.
- You're more resilient than you used to be. Despite the challenges you might face, you will find it easier to know how to deal with them and 'bounce back' to your normal routine.
- Your mind is getting sharper. There is evidence that exercise helps you think clearer and perform mental tasks such as paying attention, planning and coordinating, and decision-making. Noticing increased cognitive function and less brain fog is a sure sign of success.
- Your clothes fit better. If your clothing size is decreasing, or you find yourself able to wear clothing that was once unable to get past your shoulders, count this as a sign of success.

- You have an enhanced sense of well-being. One of the most important ways to examine our health is to assess the way we feel. A few signs to look out for include feeling better for an extended period of time, getting sick less often, feeling calmer and more balanced; and not feeling like you're on an emotional rollercoaster. An enhanced sense of well-being is proof that those workout sessions are finally paying off.

- Your mental clarity is improving. It is important to note that weight is only one aspect of our overall health. Our wellness involves not only our physical well-being, but our mental betterment as well. An improvement in overall health can be measured by enhanced mental sharpness and functioning. This includes less brain fog, the ability to think more clearly, decreased symptoms associated with anxiety and depression, and greater mental space to focus on things that matter most. Improved physical fitness could also mean better body image and decreased preoccupation with food and body image concerns.

- You are sleeping well. Falling asleep, staying asleep, and waking up feeling rested is another way to assess your improvements. Sleep is essential for so many aspects of good health… from clearing out stress hormones like cortisol to regulating blood sugar levels. Getting quality sleep is a worthwhile goal, and increased physical activity and improved nutrition can help make it possible.

- You are taking less medication. Depending on your health conditions and goals, you may be able to look to your medicine cabinet or pillbox to measure your accomplishments. People with chronic diseases such as high blood pressure, diabetes, or high cholesterol should look at a decrease in blood pressure, A1c levels, or LDL cholesterol as markers of progress. More importantly, a decrease in medication should be viewed as success as well.

- You have a healthy glow. You can learn a lot about yourself just from the state of your skin. Rashes, viral flare-ups and acne can all be signs of imbalance or inflammation in the body. Eating a healthy balanced meals, staying well-hydrated and getting enough sleep can contribute to healthy cells. Also known as…a healthier you.

Remember, finding success at anything is hard work. Continue to measure your wins in different ways as you move towards a change for the better.

The Necessary Foundation You've Discovered

Exercise is a necessity. That is a bold, but true statement. What we gain from living an active lifestyle is priceless. From the release of endorphins that help our mental state to the prevention of disease, our bodies need daily exercise to be healthy. Often, we only think of exercise when it comes to weight loss, but with this mentality, you miss out on many of the other benefits exercise offers. While losing weight is certainly a key goal to being healthy, regular exercise will also improve your overall well-being. Become familiar with how your mind communicates with your body. This relationship is key to your fitness journey. Focus on how good you feel when it is done. Think about the years you could be adding to your life. Visualize your body improving each time you work out. These pillars are a part of the foundation that will provide strength for you.

The Four Pillars

Understanding the four pillars is a must if we truly seek total wellness. Imbalances lead to brokenness, and we desire is to be whole. When your four pillars are strong and stable, you are consequently better. Let's look at them below:

1. Mental conditioning,

2. Spiritual cleansing.

3. Physical fitness.

4. Good nutrition.

These pillars are the key ingredients to a well-balanced body.

The mind must be healthy for good thoughts to flow and strong enough to weather any storm. The spirit of a man should be cleaned daily through the simple act of forgiveness. This is a true detox for the soul. Your body wants to move, so physical fitness is a gateway to longevity. Good nutrition is essential to help maintain proper bodily function, and it is an antidote to combat disease. All four components work in a synergistic form to develop a better person and a healthier body. The four pillars are a symbol of strength and stability. It is also a reflection of wholeness and total wellness.

Which of these four pillars needs the most improvement in your life?

As you continue to ponder the strength and stability of your four pillars, remember fitness is multifaceted.

If you need more reasons to practice your exercise stick-to-itiveness, here are 25 of them:

1. Decreased cardiovascular disease.

2. Better management and prevention of diabetes.

3. Improved insulin sensitivity.

4. Improved glucose metabolism.

5. Reduction in blood pressure/hypertension.

6. Decreased total cholesterol.

7. Increased energy levels.

8. Improved HDL (good cholesterol)

9. Lessens the risk of having a stroke.

10. Lower incidence of breast cancer.

11. Decreased incidence of colon cancer.

12. Lower incidence of multiple myeloma cancers.

13. Improved bone mineral density-decreasing the risk of developing osteoporosis.

14. Better musculoskeletal health.

15. Improved sarcopenia (age-related loss of muscle mass and strength)

16. Improved body composition (lean weight vs. fat weight)

17. Decreased risk of developing obesity.

18. Increased function and mobility for arthritis sufferers.

19. Reduction in stress.

20. Enhanced Mood.

21. Enhanced Self Esteem.

22. Reduced levels of depression.

23. Decreased levels of anxiety.

24. Decreased incidence of other cancers.

25. Increased metabolic rate.

Mindset Reminder

Thank you for arriving here. I know you have come a long way. Take a quick look back, and now refocus on what's in front of you. Congratulations! You have a new mindset about exercise and life. Here's a gift just for you.

I Applied

To have information is not the same as applying it. I want to see you win, so I am encouraging you to take what you know about improving your fitness and apply it. In fact, from this moment forward, the phrase "I applied" is your new affirmation. This gives you reason and cause for celebrating along the way. I applied and produced a result, I applied and became better. I applied and lost the needed weight, I applied and increased my personal value, I applied, so I could be stronger for a longer time. Not only that, but I applied to strengthen my mind, I now know I can win, I applied, again and again.

I Thrived

You have acted in key areas of your life, including improving your health and fitness, and now you are empowered to continue. After each victory or milestone celebrated, utter these words, "I thrived". Surviving is a state of mind, so too is thriving. Since I have a choice, I want to thrive. I thrived at showing myself compassion, and I thrived when self-love became important. I thrived because I scheduled my workouts and didn't cancel on my fitness. Furthermore, I thrived because I had a reason, a purpose, and a plan. I have proof that it does not matter what the goal is, fitness makes me better. I have applied and I know I have thrived. Lastly, I will leave it in the present, "I am thriving".

A Definition

I really like the word betterment as it is applicable to any aspect of life. I know it is a part of your mental makeup and journey.

Betterment is the act or process of improving something. Congratulations on getting better!

Action Steps:

1. Give yourself credit for acting.
2. Celebrate along the way.
3. Continue to apply.

"When I learn, I am able to earn. Not just money, but wisdom and honey. Wisdom is not wise until it is applied."

JOURNEY EIGHT:

REAL STORIES, REAL EXPERIENCES

All names in this chapter are pseudonyms.

A fitness journey is always unique to each individual for various reasons, so we wanted to get the thoughts and words of some of these unique people. Their stories might be similar to yours, or maybe you gain some wisdom from what they've shared.

First up is James, he works in an academic setting. He's a father, husband, and mentor.

1. When you hear the phrase "Love yourself," what does it mean to you as it relates to your health and fitness?

When I hear the phrase "love yourself" within the context of health and fitness, I currently think about the outside aesthetic appearance of a person's physique as well as how healthy that person's body is internally. I never really considered health and fitness outside the 1 credit that was required for high school graduation. However, as I have gotten older, more educated, and surrounded myself with people who have these conversations, I find myself more interested in the topic, and therefore, I have found myself more in tuned with my body. Consequently, I work out more and make concerted efforts to eliminate certain foods from my diet (especially saturated fats). Taking a more serious approach to health and fitness is beneficial for my life and my children. What I mean by this is that I consider my children in terms of staying alive as long as possible to ensure they have a stable life. Moreover, they give me the motivation to live a long and prosperous life. Growing up, my family did not discuss health and fitness as it relates to personal wellness, longevity, or even how health and fitness is connected to success in life. What I failed to mention earlier is the fact that (whether absolute or constructed truth), professional success or entrepreneurial growth is connected to how well people take care of themselves as well as their appearances. I can personally attest that proper exercise and eating gives people the energy they need to pursue and obtain their goals. Not to mention, we live in a society where appearance matters.

2. How many times have you stopped and started on your fitness journey? What was different this last time as you made a drastic change in your physical appearance?

In high school, I was a 3-sport letterman. I played football, basketball, and baseball. I was always active and engaging in physical activity. Likewise, I used to think that being healthy and fit was all about physique, lifting heavy weights, and having stamina. I did not think about the diet side of health, which is a different ball game. I never really paid attention to my eating habits because I could eat as much of what I wanted (mostly unhealthy) and still manage a great physique. When we are young, we think we are invincible, so we eat whatever we want and engage in other stupid endeavors. Because I was an athlete, my body was in shape and that's all that mattered. After high school, and when it was not a requirement to work out, I did not have a structured workout routine, and I would work out here and there. Now that I am older with children, I take health more seriously because I found myself overweight for my height and my blood work results were undesirable. Therefore, I knew I had to make a change. So, I found a personal trainer to hold me accountable and receive a structured workout and diet plan. I recently made a drastic change from not working out to working out 6-7 days a week now since July 2021. I went from 232 to 186 pounds. Although still much work, for the most part, I have changed my eating habits.

3. We often speak about mental conditioning; how did your mental makeup play a role and will continue to play a role on your journey to fitness and betterment?

Mental conditioning plays a critical role in changing my lifestyle. While I have not mastered it completely, I do feel as if I have a great command on my exercise routines, conditioning, and what I decide to eat (or not eat). For me, mental conditioning is a key component to achieving my fitness goals because it provides me with the discipline, positive self-talk, motivation, and willpower needed to remain committed to my goals. I continue to develop my mental conditioning, but what kick-started my training is surrounding myself with a community of people or resources who frequently discuss the same goals you have. Additionally, I had to seek research and self-help books to learn more insight about the purpose and benefits of improving one's lifestyle. It also feels good to NOT be the only person in the pool with a white tee-shirt on. I found that once I developed a routine, my mental conditioning evolved my spirit and will towards working out as an expectation that is not incorporated into my life. In other words, I expect to work out daily and if not, I feel guilty.

4. You are a doctoral leader in education; what demands do you face daily, and how has fitness and wellness played a role in helping you in this position? Wholeness is the goal, but you can't be whole unless you are well. How do you advocate for a holistic approach for the students you lead, educate, and inspire?

The demands that I have daily requires my attendance at work, the ability to present to various people in school or the community, and being able to help others realize their strengths, the connection between education and success after school. As a counselor, my responsibility mandates that I work with people to set action plans and build up their critical thinking skills so that they can obtain their goals. It would be hypocritical of me to engage in this work, and I cannot model the behavior or set examples accordingly. Improving my lifestyle has given me more energy and mental clarity. Therefore, I wake up early looking to attend work and while on the job, I feel more coherent. I know this has something to do with my diet because I am eating more plant-based foods and I have cut out meat for at least three months now. I am vegan now, but I am not saying that I will remain vegan. However, I know that I will not go back to eating meat three times a day every day. That much consumption is not healthy. I employed this diet so that I could lower my cholesterol levels, and I have achieved that in just three months—my blood work came back "normalized" in all categories.

5. What were some of the challenges you faced during your transformation? Who was in your corner as a support system, and how did they help you? Give me some achievements you documented during this process?

The main challenges I faced was myself. Literally, I would make every excuse in the book for not going to the gym or working out, and when Covid-19 occurred and gyms shut down, that was even more of a justification for me not to go or workout. Aside from me making excuses, ignorance would prevail. And what I mean by this is that now I know a gym is not necessarily needed to exercise because one can exercise from his or her home. I always thought you needed elaborate equipment, but you do not; people can use their own body weight, calisthenics, or run at home or around the neighborhood. Outside my trainer, I really did not depend on anyone else as a support system. Again, I would view YouTube fitness videos, read, and research. This kept me accountable and entertained. I was my biggest obstacle. I was also my own biggest advocate because when I dropped pounds weekly, it motivated me to remain consistent with the program.

6. Barring anything outside your control, will you ever quit fitness again? If no, how can you be certain? What tools will you continue to use for a stronger mind and body?

I am at the point in my life where working out 6-7 days out of the week is expected. This has become my routine. I am getting older, so I know that I need to prioritize my health and fitness and will continue to do so as long as I can physically do it. I will never quit fitness again because I have a better understanding of how to work out in various settings with limited or no equipment. Additionally, considering that eating habits are a major part of health and fitness, I will continue to make concerted efforts to eat for nutrition.

7. What advice would you give to others about not quitting and staying the course with their fitness?

The advice I would give others is in bullet points

- *Visit your doctor, get all your blood work done. This will give you a snapshot of your health and can give you a starting point for what to focus on. For me, it was lowering my cholesterol which if I had never gone to the doctor, I would still be out here eating meat three times a day almost every day.*

- *Consult a dietitian and trainer. Yes, trainers cost money, but at least pay one for a couple of months until you get a solid routine down. Write everything down and track progress.*
- *When people say diet is probably 80-90 percent of being healthy and fit, they are not lying. You need to get serious about your diet because what you consume today will rear its ugly head the older you get. Stop following that old superstition, saying things like, well, my mother survived, and we survived—cut it!*
- *I recommend meal prepping, and you will need to invest in a scale to weigh your food. You need to weigh your food (remember to consult a trainer or dietician or learn how to measure your food based on your body type, macros, protein intake, etc.). Moreover, research and consult about food variety. It does not have to be boring. This is important because we trick ourselves and end up cheating, which can kill any progress made at that point.*
- *Work out! Start off with achievable goals. For example, when I started, I began working out 3 days a week now, I work out 6-7 days.*
- *You will need to develop patience because it will take time to transform your body externally and internally. I did not see a physical change until around the 6th week (note everybody is different, so I can vary, but I do know this is not a quick process).*

- *On the days you do not feel up to working out, you must do something. I used to just get up and make it to the gym—just get there, you'd be amazed how your adrenal jolts once you arrive and get to stretching, warming up, etc. Do not take days off unless it's in your plan.*

As you can tell, James had his share of ups and downs on his fitness journey, but he has found consistency by learning to love the process and the results. Up next is a Caribbean-American engineer who lost 100 pounds, but it wasn't a cakewalk. Natonya shares some insight about her journey.

1. First, congratulations on joining the century club for weight loss. This is a great testament to your dedication to improving your overall health. How does it make you feel to know you accomplished a goal of this size?

I feel great! I know this is something that I worked hard at over an almost 2-year period, and it feels great to reach this milestone.

2. How many times previously had you attempted a weight loss journey, and what was different this time?

Too many times to count. It finally clicked that I didn't have to be perfect. In previous attempts, I would "mess up" and go off the rails because I was expecting perfection. On my desk now is a post-it that says, "Consistency over perfection." This approach has been the big change for me. I give myself the grace to have a meal (sometimes 2… or a weekend) in a day that may not be in the plan and to get up the next day and get back to the plan. Working with a fitness coach also played a major part. This gave me the accountability I needed (and still need) to get up and move. I could always cancel going to the gym with my friend at the last minute. But when I was paying for someone's time and canceling at the last minute meant paying for time and not receiving the service, I got my butt to the gym. The accountability extended past the time in the gym to check-ins on eating and exercise outside our scheduled times. This also helped to keep me on track.

3. We talk about mindset all the time; what was your thought process during some difficult times on your weight loss journey? Did you think about giving up?

The "consistency over perfection" approach was the major mindset shift for me (see above). Weight loss does have a large impact on your mental and emotional state. Every so often, it requires isolation to stay focused (especially if your friend circle is not on the same journey or doesn't yet know how to support you). These were some of the hardest times — passing up going out because I knew that if I did, I wouldn't make supportive food choices. Did you think about giving up? Of course! I tried… but I kept going. Having a personal fitness coach who understood the highs and lows of the journey and could motivate me at the times I needed it most helped greatly.

4. What other areas of your overall health have seen an improvement after losing 100 pounds? Did you see improvements in heart rate, blood pressure, cholesterol, etc.?

My resting heart rate is now in the 60s… the first time I saw it, I thought I was dying and had to google what was going on 😅.
This is a good thing! I've also seen improvements in my blood pressure and my A1C is now out of the "pre-diabetic" range.
5. When it comes to nutrition, what worked for you? Was it more about a lifestyle change, or were you tempted by fad diets?

It was definitely more about a lifestyle changed. From past attempts, I knew that complete deprivation of anything did not work for me. I saw a nutritionist who educated me on the plate method and this is basically what I've stuck to. I started out trying to meet a 1600 calorie a day intake by counting calories and recording meals. This worked for a while, but I had to stop counting calories because I was feeling very defeated in the days I went over. Now I follow the plate method.
I also find it helpful to meal prep. It's less likely that I'll be tempted to purchase a quick unhealthy meal if I know I have food prepared at home.
6. You are from the Caribbean islands and many celebrations are around food. How do you handle that with continuing the next leg of your journey?

This has been a challenge and continues to be! I was really aware of it last year when I was home for the holidays and realized that my family kept bringing me food! It was their way of showing love. Food being a part of celebrations also extends to my circle of friends.

Moderation is key. Remembering that 1 "bad" meal doesn't mean that I throw away years of hard work. Furthermore, we are encouraging each other with activity instead of food-based celebrations. Lastly, it's ok to say "no, I won't be able to attend" or "no, thank you. I've had enough."

7. What intangible things did you get from working with a professional fitness coach?

Because weight loss has mental and emotional components, my professional fitness coach sometimes functioned as a therapist, motivator, supporter, and cheerleader.

This is some great advice for those of you seeking weight loss on your fitness journey. Notice, this was a two-year process for Natonya. She didn't quit.

Let's see what the journey of Logan has been like. She is a soon-to-be college graduate that adopted fitness as a lifestyle during her senior year of high school.

1. For so many people, fitness is a slippery slope. How did you get into fitness and for what reasons?

To me, fitness is a lifelong journey. In middle school and early high school, I was an active student-athlete. Then, as my classes got harder, and I approached college application season, I dropped to only focusing on schoolwork. At that point, I didn't focus on working out and being active at all. A year passed, and my dad often mentioned Antonio and his killer workouts. He convinced me to tag along. I found myself jogging in the cold to the neighborhood gym, where we'd meet Antonio and the other members of "Boot Camp." It's safe to say that I was hooked. Antonio's workouts had the elements I love of sports, including the team comradery to organized workouts.

I got into fitness the second time because of the strength it gave me, physically and mentally. I remember completing a sweaty workout one morning and exclaiming to Antonio that I finally had abs! More than that, I felt like I had a secret weapon. Fitness gives me time to focus on challenging and bettering myself each day. Going to the gym gives me time to relax and also to motivate myself. Holding yourself accountable to showing up for yourself can take you incredibly far… and the abs are a nice bonus.

2. During your senior year of high school, you would workout at 5:45am consistently 3-4 times per week; what gave you the motivation to work out before school? How did it help you as a student? Did you ever think of giving up on your fitness?

A 5 am wake-up call for a 6 am workout sure woke me up, and it was so worth it. Ever since starting with Antonio, I have not quit my fitness journey. Often, I want to roll over and punch the snooze button, but think about how good I'd feel after it kept me going. Working out with a plan changes everything. I'm not convinced that I was alert enough to come up with something to do in the gym on my own. I love being able to just show up and have a killer plan awaiting me. Working out smarter, not harder, made me feel like I was getting the best experience possible. I was not jumping around for 30 minutes; instead, I was following a set plan from a professional.

3. You are now in your senior year of college; what transferred over from experience previously mentioned? How often did you work out in college? What non-fitness-related challenges have you faced that your commitment to fitness has helped you with?

Yes, I am now a graduating senior at the University of North Carolina! I've kept up an active lifestyle throughout college. I found workouts that made me happy— swimming, cycling classes, and traditional weight training. My time of day to work out varied by semester. I found myself at the gym at 10 pm, lunchtime, or early morning depending on my schedule. As long as I made it happen, I was happy. I aim to work out with weights 4-5 days a week. On the weekends, I try for low-intensity, steady-state workouts such as walking or hiking. Working out gave me an outlet to work off stress. When I faced challenges, I knew I was controlling at least one thing, my fitness. My gym time was non-negotiable, no matter how busy I got. I've never regretted a workout. When my earbuds went in, the stress melted away. The stair machine (also known as The Monster) is wonderful to sweat off a midterm or term paper! My longtime boyfriend, Drew, is also passionate about fitness. Having a buddy helps keep me motivated. We met my first week of college and went on one of our first dates at the gym. We studied abroad in Singapore together and continued training there. Now that we are at home due to COVID-19 pandemic, we work out from home or outdoors.

4. On a scale of 1-10, with 1 being the lowest and 10 the highest, how confident are you now? What about before you started living a fit lifestyle?

Before working out, I felt like I was taller and larger than my peers. My confidence was probably at 5/10 at times. Now that I have fitness in my life, I'd say I'm an 8/10 for confidence. A 9/10 or 10/10 on a good day!

5. When you hear our strategy, "Love yourself enough to love yourself some more," what comes to mind for you? Has loving yourself ever been a challenge for you? If so, what are some things you did or said to strengthen this relationship?

I love your strategy! You can't pour from an empty cup, so it's important to me to proactive self-compassion. I'm a better daughter, student, employee, girlfriend, and more when I'm active. I feel like my greatest strength and weakness are the same: my sensitivity. Surprisingly, I felt more emotional and out of control before starting regular workouts. We only get one body, so taking care of my body is a priority. Another thing that helped me feel better is properly fueling my body. Nutrition matters, but doesn't have to be boring. Fueling yourself with lean proteins (I'm a pescetarian!), plus veggies, fruit, carbs, and healthy fats, is a form of self-love. I aim for the 80/20 rule. To me, this means nutritious foods most of the time with plenty of room for fun. Coffee, waffles, and wine are all part of a normal week for me.

6. Mental conditioning is important no matter your journey. What are some things you do and say to condition your mind daily?

Mind over matter
Show up every day
Make fitness your "me" time
Motivate yourself in new ways… could I try changing up my workout today, such as working out outdoors or shifting the time of day?
Make "someday" today
The feeling after will be worth it

7. What advice would you give to other high school and college students that may not be athletes about the importance of fitness and healthy living?

Make it fun —work out with a partner, group, or with great music. Others can motivate you! Reward yourself for hitting your goals. Maybe buying a new pair of sneakers or nice leggings to wear to the gym. Make it as easy as possible. For me, this looks like following a workout plan created by a professional. Just show up and get it done. You can accomplish a lot in a short time, and the benefits will spread into every area of your life. I also enjoy functional fitness and changing things up. Don't be scared to get started! Your future self will thank you.

Finally, we will get some insight from a busy CEO. Barry is great at leading his company and the 3500 employees who serve their customers. He is also great at sticking to his fitness commitments even while juggling family, work, and community help.

1. As a busy CEO, where do you find the time to consistently workout three or more times per week? Was fitness always an important area for you?

Well, I've always been lean and somewhat athletic, but never took fitness serious until years later. I remember speaking with a friend, and he mentioned how working out at 5am 4 mornings a week changed his mind and body. This intrigued me, so I started a journey that I've been on for 12 years now, and I can honestly say I've only missed 5 scheduled workouts during this time. I am a better father, husband, and leader because of an improved health and fitness life.

2. To have that level of consistency working out, a strong mindset has to be a major ingredient for you. Has mental strength helped you in your journey?

I have always taking pride in being humble, leading by example, and having a strong desire to succeed, so yes, the mental aspect is important to anything I do. Early morning workouts are best for me due to my work schedule, so I don't allow excuses for not getting it done every Monday,

Tuesday, Thursday, and Friday. This was a mental challenge for me, but now it's my strength.

3. Twelve years is a long time on a fitness journey. Did you ever think about giving it up? What motivates you to keep going?

Quitting is usually not an option for me once I've started something. There are surely days, I'd rather stay in bed than workout, thankfully I don't act on that thought, but it's a normal one to have on a fitness journey. As it relates to what motivates me to keep going, I would say family, personal growth, and my commitment to our associates at the company provides plenty of motivation.

4. How does self-love play a role in what you do daily? What type of workouts do you engage in to keep things interesting?

I never really gave much thought to the phrase "self-love" until I heard it mentioned at a wellness event for company employees. Often times as givers, we just give and become immune to everything else until we realize our cup is empty. This is one reason fitness is so important to me. I can refill my cup and keep helping others. When it comes to workouts, my fitness coach keeps me inspired with a combination of exercises, progressions, and creativity to keep boredom at bay. Personally, I love functional workouts with cardio segments built in.

5. Since you are big into health and fitness, what is the wellness culture like at your company?

As you can probably imagine, it's competitive. We encourage total wellness for our associates and do our best to provide the needed resources to help make it possible. We have an onsite fitness center; monthly lunch n learn classes, mental health coaches, and more. If our associates are healthy, they are better at serving our clients and as a result, the company is healthier. Everyone has a role to play, and it starts with me.

6. You mentioned a conversation with a friend piqued your interest. When you started in fitness, what was your reason (why)?

I was under a lot of stress with the growth of the company, and I wasn't managing it well. The one thing that stood out from that conversation was "mind and body." I guess you can say stress management resource for over a decade now, and truthfully for the rest of my life if I have any say so.

7. Thank you for taking the time to share some insight into your fitness journey. What advice would you give to those wanting to stick with fitness?

Take some self-care for your cup so that you can pour more into the cup of others. It's what I did, and it hasn't stopped working for me yet.

Barry shared some important points about his journey that I hope encourages you to stick with your fitness or anything else that is important to you because you are outstanding and so are our bodies.

Did you know our bodies are amazing machines? Seriously,

Just Think About This…

Do you ever ponder how miraculous

Your body truly is?

For example, under your flesh

(and including your flesh) are 11

incredible systems, each more

complex than a super-computer.

Here they are:

Integumentary System (hair, skin, and nails)

Skeletal System (bones)

Muscular System (muscles, tendons, ligaments)

Nervous System (brain, spinal cord)

Endocrine System (glands and hormones)

Circulatory System (heart, blood, veins)

Lymphatic System (lymph vessels, debris removal)

Respiratory System (lungs, oxygen)

Digestive System (mouth, stomach, intestines)

Urinary System (kidneys, bladder, fluid)

Reproductive Systems (male, female)

And, these systems are all integrated,

synchronized and seamlessly working

with each other 100% automatically,

non-stop, 24/7. It's incredible when,

you stop and think about it.

The Amazing YOU!

The warm-up, the workout, and the cool-down is about you. This journey you are on is also about you, the growth mindset, a commitment to betterment, and your toughness is about you as well. No matter the goals or which side of the mountain you decide to climb, it's about you, but not only about you. Keep that in mind!

Closing arguments

While the benefits of fitness have long been advertised, this is a mental battle we are facing as well. If we don't get this part right, we miss an integral part of the journey and the benefits of fitness go overlooked or undervalued. The reality is…you can't quit! Close your eyes for 30 seconds, and breathe slowly and deeply before reading these final words by former Marine Jeremy Stalnecker.

We can't quit because

1. We can't quit because of the sacrifices of others.

The truth in this is simple and yet very direct. Life is not about you or only about what you are dealing with now. There are people who have gone before you that sacrificed, some even giving up their lives, so that you could do something great with yours. To allow your past to keep you from moving forward or decide that things are just too hard is to say that the sacrifices of others are meaningless. Live and accomplish in such a way that the crowd of witnesses, those who have gone before you, are proud of the life that you are living and would not consider their sacrifice on your behalf a waste.

2. We can't quit because the stakes are high.

What is really at stake if you decide to quit on what you once decided was important? If you give up on a dream or decide that being a person of character and integrity is just too hard? The stakes are really high, yet I think we rarely look outside ourselves when we make the decision to give up. It is not about you; it is about the generations of people that your decision to either press on or give up will impact. Before you quit, ask this question and honestly answer, "Who will be impacted by my decision to stop doing what I once decided was important?"

3. We can't quit because we have been uniquely gifted to finish the race.

The temptation to quit, can at times, be overwhelming. When those times come, before you give up, take a minute to step back and ask "why". The answers won't make the road ahead easier, but they will make it worthwhile. Decide to do something great. Get started. Ignore the voice that tells you it would be easier to quit. Live a life the makes a difference.

Remember, winning is a self-fulfilling prophecy: if you decide to be a success, you can be.

Building your confidence is an evolving process that starts by saying to yourself, "I believe I can win."

About the Author

Antonio Evans is a fitness entrepreneur and motivational coach that has spent years inspiring people from all walks of life. He is the founder of the fitness brands Plank Life, Power Wheel Race, and Hustle your Health. Antonio is the owner of ReShape Fitness LLC, where he has been providing fitness and wellness services to communities, organizations, and individuals for 15 years. He created the Making Fitness Fun and Educational program geared toward middle school kids. Antonio is a passionate and energetic speaker with an eagerness to deliver applicable lessons. Antonio has spoken at various colleges, presented at different conferences, and inspired many groups. He's the author of the motivational book 100 Things to Ponder and his upcoming book Funny Workout Stories. Antonio featured his industry knowledge in the book How to Open and Operate a Financially Successful Personal Training Business. He was also featured in a national commercial for Visit Pittsburgh. Antonio has authored more than 200 motivational quotes that inspire people daily. Antonio is a University of South Carolina Aiken graduate with a degree in Exercise Science and has been a leader in the fitness industry for 20 years. He was the first Exercise Science alumni to serve as commencement speaker for the university. Antonio mentors young men using fitness, baseball, and entrepreneurship as teaching tools.

You can follow Antonio on Instagram @antoniodevans and Twitter @antonioevans21

www.AntoniodEvans.com